WORDS OF WISDOM

For The Power-Filled Life

Daily TREASURES

PAULA WHITE

© 2004 by Paula White Ministries

ISBN 0-9712650-6-2

Scripture quotations are taken from the King James Version of the Bible unless
otherwise specified.

Published by Paula White Ministries, a Media Ministry of Without Walls International Church Inc., P.O. Box 25151, Tampa FL 33622-5151 www.paulawhite.org

PAULA WHITE
M I N I S T R I E S
TRANSFORMING LIVES • HEALING HEARTS • WINNING SOULS

Printed by Plus Communications, St Louis, Missouri

Table of Contents

Dedication

First, I dedicate this book to my Lord and Savior Jesus Christ, who daily loads me with "treasures" (Psalm 68:19). Thank you, Father, for choosing me. Words will never be adequate to articulate my love and desire for you.

To my husband, my coach, my best friend and my pastor – Randy. You are a rare gem that grows more precious each day. Thank you for seeing the diamond in me when all I saw was coal. You are my joy and the wind that allows me to soar. My love for you is indescribable.

To my four children - Bradley, Brandon, Kristen, and Angie. Your unyielding love and support go far beyond anything I could ever ask for. Thank you for trusting in the vision as much as I did and standing beside me to support the call of God on our lives. You are my joy.

And to my World Partners. Without you, Paula White Ministries would not be what it is today! Thank you for believing in a "messed up Mississippi girl" with a big God and a big dream. Together we will transform lives, heal hearts, and win souls. Great will be your reward! I believe in you!

Introduction

Daily Treasures is a collection of powerful truths and gems of knowledge from preacher, teacher, motivator and "midwife to dreams" - Paula White. It will bless you daily with nuggets of wisdom on topics ranging from Faith to Failure and Decision-making to Destiny. Relevant scriptures reveal God's thoughts on each topic as Paula imparts wisdom to strengthen your spirit and enhance your daily walk with God.

That the God of our Lord Jesus Christ, the Father of glory, may give to you the spirit of wisdom and revelation in the knowledge of Him, the eyes of your understanding being enlightened; that you may know what is the hope of His calling, what are the riches of the glory of His inheritance in the saints, and what is the exceeding greatness of His power toward us who believe, according to the working of His mighty power.

Ephesians 1:17-19

Goal Setting & Preparation

Set goals that make you rely on God.

Habakkuk 1

[5] Behold ye among the heathen, and regard, and wonder marvelously: for I will work a work in your days which ye will not believe, though it be told you.

_____

_____

_____

_____

_____

Purpose in your heart to strive to achieve something that would never be possible without God's help. That's how you can provoke Him to "show off" in your life.

Goal Setting & Preparation

You eat an elephant one bite at a time.

Galatians 6
[9] And let us not be weary in well doing: for in due season we shall reap, if we faint not.

_____

_____

_____

_____

_____

Map your success. Approach each step as a separate mission,
and you will eventually arrive at the end of the goal.

Goal Setting & Preparation

Don't make a decision with limited information

2 Timothy 3

[16] All scripture is given by inspiration of God, and is profitable for doctrine, for reproof, for correction, for instruction in righteousness.

_____

_____

_____

_____

_____

In addition to weighing all of your options, search the Word of God for answers to any questions in your life. Therein lies the key to your success.

Goal Setting & Preparation

When you write down a goal, you increase the percentage of achieving it 90 times

Habakkuk 2

2 And the LORD answered me, and said, Write the vision, and make it plain upon tables, that he may run that readeth it.

_____

_____

_____

_____

_____

Writing down your goals not only reminds you of your vision, but it declares boldly to the enemy that you are serious about achieving it.

Goal Setting & Preparation

In choosing to undertake a project, look at four things –
(1) Did God tell you to do it?
(2) Is there a creative challenge?
(3) Will there be pleasure and passion in doing it?
(4) Is it profitable?

1 Corinthians 14
[40] Let all things be done decently and in order.

_____

_____

_____

_____

_____

*Systematically approach each opportunity to ensure that you are making the best use of
your time and remaining aligned with God's vision for you.*

Goal Setting & Preparation

Build an ark and let the rain catch up to your vision

Genesis 6

13 And God said unto Noah, … 14 Make thee an ark…

22 Thus did Noah; according to all that God commanded him…

Genesis 7

17 And the flood was forty days upon the earth; and the waters increased, and bare up the ark, and it was lift up above the earth.

_____

_____

_____

_____

_____

What are you waiting for? God's ability to manifest His divine destiny in your life can be limited by your lack of willingness to MOVE into that destiny!

Goal Setting & Preparation

If you don't know where you are going,
you are already there

Proverbs 3

⁶ In all thy ways acknowledge him, and he shall direct thy paths.

_____

_____

_____

_____

_____

Direction will not be made clear until you seek God's wisdom and desire for you.
If He's not driving, you're either in REVERSE or PARK.

Goal Setting & Preparation

If you fail to plan, you plan to fail

2 Chronicles 12

[14]   And he did evil, because he prepared not his heart to seek the LORD.

_____

_____

_____

_____

_____

God has a divine plan for your life. So should you. If you wander without a Godly purpose, a
fleshly one will create itself for you.

Goal Setting & Preparation

Seek God to make you effective

Isaiah 58

2 Yet they seek me daily, and delight to know my ways, as a nation that did righteousness, and forsook not the ordinance of their God: they ask of me the ordinances of justice; they take delight in approaching to God.

_____

_____

_____

_____

_____

As you seek after God and His plan for you, He will begin to bless your undertakings and direct you to the path He has laid for you.

Goal Setting & Preparation

Initiate your blessing. Nothing significant will
happen until you initiate it

Ecclesiastes 5
[3] For a dream cometh through the multitude of business...

_____

_____

_____

_____

_____

*Until you "work your stuff", God won't "work His". Get to work today to not only
find your vision, but to also achieve it.*

Goal Setting & Preparation

God has a prepared place for prepared people.
The difficulty is not preparing the place but the people.

John 14
[2] In my Father's house are many mansions…I go to prepare a place for you.

Are you ready to go where God wants to take you? If He called on you today, what would it take to be ready? Cut off hindrances today so that God can get busy in your life.

Goal Setting & Preparation

Only three people out of 100 plan a day. If you can't plan a day, you can't plan a lifetime.

Exodus 24
4   And Moses wrote all the words of the LORD, and rose up early in the morning, and builded an altar under the hill, and twelve pillars, according to the twelve tribes of Israel.

_____

_____

_____

_____

_____

Moses took direction from God, wrote down the plan, and began to implement it.
Take a lesson from Moses today as you map out your day and your life.

Treasure of the Day   *Paula White*

Goal Setting & Preparation

The moment you start to prepare – you serve notice that
you are going somewhere.

1 Corinthians 9
[24] Know ye not that they which run in a race run all, but one receiveth the prize?
So run, that ye may obtain.

_____

_____

_____

_____

_____

Start running toward your divine destiny today to declare to the enemy that you are in it to win it!.

Goal Setting & Preparation

Information is power – Never make a decision with limited information

Proverbs 19

2 Also, that the soul be without knowledge, it is not good; and he that hasteth
with his feet sinneth

_____

_____

_____

_____

_____

When you fail to research all of your options, you give the power to choose away.

Goal Setting & Preparation

God is not intimidated by your aspirations.
He gave them to you – so go for it.

John 14

[12] Verily, verily, I say unto you, He that believeth on me, the works that I do shall he do also; and greater works than these shall he do; because I go unto my Father.

_____

_____

_____

_____

_____

Our sovereign God who can do all things has created you in His image. Through Him, you can achieve more than you are even able to imagine – even greater works than Jesus did!

Goal Setting & Preparation

Go confidently in the direction of your dreams. Live the
life you imagined.

Joshua 14

[9] And Moses sware on that day, saying, Surely the land whereon thy feet have
trodden shall be thine inheritance, and thy children's for ever, because thou hast
wholly followed the LORD my God.

_____

_____

_____

_____

_____

*To follow God is to follow your dreams and walk the path to your destiny. Step out on
faith and He will catch you.*

Goal Setting & Preparation

Success only comes before work in the dictionary.

2 Timothy 2

[15] Study to shew thyself approved unto God, a workman that needeth not to be ashamed, rightly dividing the word of truth.

_____

_____

_____

_____

_____

Can God trust you with the vision He has designed for your life. Prove your diligence to Him now by taking the time to study His Word and understand His heart.

Goal Setting & Preparation

You are only as strong publicly as you are privately.

Matthew 26

[36] Then cometh Jesus with them unto a place called Gethsemane, and saith unto the disciples, Sit ye here, while I go and pray yonder.

_____

_____

_____

_____

Even Jesus began each day with private prayer and meditation to remain focused and prepare for the tasks ahead. If He who was one with God did this, how much more should you as a child of God?

Finances: Putting your money where your heart is

Audit your life and create a budget

Luke 14

28 For which of you, intending to build a tower, sitteth not down first, and counteth the cost, whether he have sufficient to finish it?

_____

_____

_____

_____

_____

The only way you can manage your money is to be diligent in tracking your spending against your earning. You'll be amazed to see how tiny frivolous purchases will add up and deplete your pocket quickly!

Finances: Putting your money where your heart is

Your checkbook is a book of revelation.

Isaiah 55
2   Wherefore do ye spend money for that which is not bread? and your labour for
that which satisfieth not? hearken diligently unto me, and eat ye that which is good,
and let your soul delight itself in fatness.

_____

_____

_____

_____

_____

Survey your checkbook ledger to see what you have been spending your money on.
It will reveal startling truths about your priorities in life.

Finances: *Putting your money where your heart is*

If you are living the Christian life and it is not abundant, then you're not living it right.

John 10

[10] … I am come that they might have life, and that they might have it more abundantly.

_____

_____

_____

_____

_____

God's wish for you is that you will live abundantly. If there is lack in your life, take an inventory to see what you may be doing (or not doing) to delay the activation of God's promise for your life.

Finances: Putting your money where your heart is

You can't see your paycheck as your source, but as your seed.

2 Corinthians 9

[10] Now he that ministereth seed to the sower both minister bread for your food, and multiply your seed sown, and increase the fruits of your righteousness)
[11] Being enriched in every thing to all bountifulness, which causeth through us thanksgiving to God.[12] For the administration of this service not only supplieth the want of the saints, but is abundant also by many thanksgivings unto God;

_____

_____

_____

_____

_____

You must shift your mindset to understand that the reason you are blessed is to bless others.
Your seed cannot be multiplied to bless anyone else until you first PLANT it.

Finances: Putting your money where your heart is

Blessing is not just money – it is the empowerment to prosper and succeed.

Deuteronomy 28

[8] The LORD shall command the blessing upon thee in thy storehouses, and in all that thou settest thine hand unto; and he shall bless thee in the land which the LORD thy God giveth thee

_____

_____

_____

_____

_____

When you are in true covenant with God and living sin-free, blessings and increase will manifest in all areas of your life – from finances, to relationships, to spiritual growth.

Finances: Putting your money where your heart is

Something supernatural will always happen when you give.

Genesis 26

[12]   Then Isaac sowed in that land, and received in the same year an hundredfold: and the LORD blessed him.

_____

_____

_____

_____

_____

Even if you don't see it immediately, you can trust that God will bless you beyond your imagination for your faithfulness in giving.

Finances: Putting your money where your heart is

Prosperity without purpose is materialism.

Proverbs 1

[32] For ... the prosperity of fools shall destroy them.

The purpose of your being blessed is not so that you can lay up earthly treasures.
It is so that you can lay up heavenly treasures by financing the kingdom and blessing others.

Finances: Putting your money where your heart is

God's presence will cause you to prosper.

Isaiah 10

27 And it shall come to pass in that day, that his burden shall be taken away from off thy shoulder, and his yoke from off thy neck, and the yoke shall be destroyed because of the anointing.

_____

_____

_____

_____

_____

The anointing to prosper is not subject to what is going on in your life. It is subject only to your ability to remain in covenant with God.

Finances: Putting your money where your heart is

Your life should be a reflection of the
condition of your soul.

3 John 1
2 Beloved, I wish above all things that thou mayest prosper and be in health,
even as thy soul prospereth.

_____

_____

_____

_____

_____

If your soul is prosperous, demand equity in every area of your life.

Finances: Putting your money where your heart is

What leaves your hand determines what leaves God's hand.

2 Corinthians 9

⁶ But this I say, He which soweth sparingly shall reap also sparingly; and he which soweth bountifully shall reap also bountifully.

_____

_____

_____

_____

_____

God has a handful of blessings just waiting for you. When you release what's in your hand, He'll release what's in His hand. Give God your very best, and He'll give you His very best.

Finances: Putting your money where your heart is

God wants to bring you out to bring you in.

Exodus 3

[17] And I have said, I will bring you up out of the affliction of Egypt unto the land of the Canaanites, and the Hittites, and the Amorites, and the Perizzites, and the Hivites, and the Jebusites, unto a land flowing with milk and honey.

_____

_____

_____

_____

_____

God will bring you out of the land of not enough (Egypt) and through the land of just enough (wilderness) and into the land of more than enough (Canaan).

Finances: Putting your money where your heart is

If it's <u>too much to give</u>, then it's <u>too much to receive</u>.

Proverbs 10

[4] He becometh poor that dealeth with a slack hand: but the hand of the diligent maketh rich.

_____

_____

_____

_____

_____

You cannot continue to pray for and expect to receive something you don't give.

Love

You cannot love others until you love yourself; you cannot truly love yourself until you know and experience God's love for you

1 John 4

7   Beloved, let us love one another: for love is of God; and every one that loveth is born of God, and knoweth God.

_____

_____

_____

_____

_____

God's love and true sacrifice for us is the ultimate example to follow in learning to love others and ourselves. It is when you experience His unconditional love that you can begin to share it with others.

Love

In the absence of recognition of real love, you will do crazy things to get someone to like or love you.

Judges 16

[6] And Delilah said to Samson, "Tell me, I pray thee, wherein thy great strength lieth, and wherewith thou mightest be bound to afflict thee." [17] …he told her all his heart, and said unto her," There hath not come a razor upon mine head…if I be shaven, then my strength will go from me, and I shall become weak, and be like any other man."

[19] And she made him sleep upon her knees; and she called for a man, and she caused him to shave off the seven locks of his head; and she began to afflict him,

_____

_____

_____

_____

_____

In an effort to impress her, Samson told Delilah exactly how to weaken him to the point of vulnerability. We all have been "fools for love" a time or two, but true agape love is available to all through the Ultimate Sacrifice that Jesus already made for us.

Love

Ultimately, fulfillment is found when you know the love of God.

Ephesians 3

[19] And to know the love of Christ, which passeth knowledge, that ye might be filled with all the fulness of God.

_____

_____

_____

_____

_____

Many people seek to be fulfilled through spouses, friends, work or money. True satisfaction and wholeness comes from knowing and communing with God.

Love

Love will never fail.

1 Corinthians 13
[7] It always protects, always trusts, always hopes, always perseveres.
[8] Love never fails. (NIV)

_____

_____

_____

_____

_____

The bible teaches us that God is love. To fully understand how powerful love is, fill in the scripture above with "God" - God always protects, always hopes, always perseveres. God never fails.

Love

Loving makes you giving.

2 Corinthians 9

[13] You will be glorifying God through your generous gifts. For your generosity to them will prove that you are obedient to the Good News of Christ. (NLT).

_____

_____

_____

_____

_____

A generous hand is an indicator of a loving heart. When we give out of a desire to help someone else, we are glorifying God by sharing His generosity.

Love

You give love the way you want love given to you.

Exodus 34

6 …The Lord! the Lord! a God merciful and gracious, slow to anger, and abundant in loving-kindness and truth…

_____

_____

_____

_____

_____

Subconsciously, we often show love to others the way that we expect it to be shown to us. Take a moment to reflect on the way that God has shown love to you, and make a conscious decision to share that love with others.

Love

God loved you when you were unlovable.

John 3

16 For God so loved the world, that he gave his only begotten Son, that whosoever believeth in him should not perish, but have everlasting life.

_____

_____

_____

_____

_____

Thousands of generations before you were born, God knew of every sin you would ever commit. Yet, in spite of that, He gave His life to exonerate you!

Love

Once you experience God's love for yourself, you will
understand that absolutely nothing can separate you from
it.

Romans 8

35 Who shall separate us from the love of Christ? shall tribulation, or distress, or
persecution, or famine, or nakedness, or peril, or sword?

38 For I am persuaded, that neither death, nor life, nor angels, nor principalities,
nor powers, nor things present, nor things to come,

39 Nor height, nor depth, nor any other creature, shall be able to separate us from
the love of God, which is in Christ Jesus our Lord.

_____

_____

_____

_____

_____

*Take a moment and revel in the fact that no matter what happens in your life,
no matter what you do, God's love is a constant that you can depend on.*

Love

Love makes you give, and lust makes you take.

1 Peter 2

[11] Dearly beloved, I beseech you as strangers and pilgrims, abstain from fleshly lusts, which war against the soul;

_____

_____

_____

_____

_____

Lust is of the flesh and can never be satisfied, no matter how much it takes.
Love is of God and can be satisfied only through true fellowship with Him.

Love

The love God has for you is unconditional, unwavering and irrevocable.

Jeremiah 31

³ The LORD hath appeared of old unto me, saying, Yea, I have loved thee with an everlasting love: therefore with lovingkindness have I drawn thee..

_____

_____

_____

_____

_____

Isn't it refreshing to know that God's love does not depend on what you do or what you look like? He is madly in love with you and nothing can ever change that.

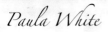

Love

The ability to love someone else comes directly from our love relationship with God.

1 John 4

21 And this commandment have we from him, That he who loveth God love his brother also.

_____

_____

_____

_____

_____

Are you in love with God? How can you show man love if you have not shared it with your creator? God has been "courting" you for all of eternity.

Love

God loves us because of who He is,
not because of who we are.

1 John 4

[10] Herein is love, not that we loved God, but that he loved us, and sent his Son to be the propitiation for our sins.

_____

_____

_____

_____

_____

God's love is everlasting and unwavering. Rest in the assurance that He is with you and loves you for all of eternity, regardless of your transgressions.

Love

Never again insult God's great sacrifice by questioning His love.

Ephesians 5

[2] And walk in love, as Christ also hath loved us, and hath given himself for us an offering and a sacrifice to God for a sweet-smelling savor.

No matter how bad your situation looks, you can trust in God's love.
Doubting Him says that you don't appreciate His sacrifice and love.

Destiny & Purpose

God gives purpose to the years of question marks in our lives.

Exodus 9

[16] And in very deed for this cause have I raised thee up, for to shew in thee my power; and that my name may be declared throughout all the earth.

_____

_____

_____

_____

_____

Although each of us has a unique and powerful purpose designated by God, we are all called to devote our lives to exemplifying God's power and might throughout the world. Our job is to figure out "how" He wants us to accomplish that task.

Destiny & Purpose

The promise is often bigger than the person.

Ephesians 3

20 Now unto him that is able to do exceeding abundantly above all that we ask or think, according to the power that worketh in us.

_____

_____

_____

_____

_____

Your dreams will be so big that they will challenge you and stretch you. That is necessary so that you have to depend on God to bring them to fruition. What good would it do to dream of something so small you could achieve it alone with little effort?

Destiny & Purpose

Definition of frustration: to settle for less than your destiny.

2 Corinthians 5

5 The Spirit of God whets our appetite by giving us a taste of what's ahead. He puts a little of heaven in our hearts so that we'll never settle for less. (MSG)

_____

_____

_____

_____

_____

What a mighty God we serve! In each of us, he has planted a tiny piece of heaven so that we may always have some sense of what we are striving toward. The frustration you feel may be because you have moved away from that end destination.

Destiny & Purpose

We were born to make manifest the glory of God that is within us.

Exodus 9

16 And in very deed for this cause have I raised thee up, for to shew in thee my power; and that my name may be declared throughout all the earth.

_____

_____

_____

_____

_____

The purpose that God has called you to will be your unique opportunity to share God's glory so that others might be saved.

Destiny & Purpose

To just exist is a waste of days.

Titus 3

[14] And let our own [people really] learn to apply themselves to good deeds (to honest labor and honorable employment), so that they may be able to meet necessary demands whenever the occasion may require and not be living idle and uncultivated and unfruitful lives. (AMP)

_____

_____

_____

_____

_____

God has given each of us a divine purpose to fulfill. We insult Him when we waste our time striving toward earthly goals, or no goals at all.

Destiny & Purpose

Whatever a person is – they were before and just didn't know it.

Ephesians 2

[10] For we are his workmanship, created in Christ Jesus unto good works, which God hath before ordained that we should walk in them.

_____

_____

_____

_____

_____

You have always been whatever God has called you to be. It was ordained before the earth was formed. Now is your time to step into that divine destiny, with confidence that our Father is leading the way!

Destiny & Purpose

Don't let your history hinder you from your destiny.

Philippians 3

[13] Brethren, I count not myself to have apprehended: but this one thing I do, forgetting those things which are behind, and reaching forth unto those things which are before…

_____

_____

_____

_____

_____

How can you focus on your point of destination if your eyes are distracted by your point of origination? Make the decision today to focus only on where God is taking you, and not where you've been.

Destiny & Purpose

To hold on to your dream and fulfill God's plan for your life, you must keep moving forward.

Philippians 3

[12] Not that I have now attained [this ideal], or have already been made perfect, but I press on to lay hold of (grasp) and make my own, that for which Christ Jesus (the Messiah) has laid hold of me and made me His own. (AMP)

Obstacles are what you see when you take your eyes off of the goal. No matter what, do not get distracted. Keep moving towards your destiny – someone else's salvation may depend on it.

Treasure of the Day　　　　　*Paula White*

Destiny & Purpose

If not now, then when? If not you, then who? The only
place to start is where you are.

Ecclesiastes 11
[4] He who observes the wind [and waits for all conditions to be favorable] will not
sow, and he who regards the clouds will not reap. (AMP)

_____

_____

_____

_____

_____

*God is calling you into your destiny NOW. He has a unique plan designed just for you that
no one else can fulfill. Don't delay your destiny another day!*

Destiny & Purpose

While you're waiting, the makings of a miracle are growing inside of you.

Habakkuk 2

[3] For the vision is yet for an appointed time and it hastens to the end [fulfillment]; it will not deceive or disappoint. Though it tarry, wait [earnestly] for it, because it will surely come; it will not be behindhand on its appointed day. (AMP)

_____

_____

_____

_____

_____

Don't get frustrated if you feel like you're in a holding pattern. God just may be repositioning things below to ensure a safe landing for you.

Destiny & Purpose

You may be in the driver's seat, but God holds the map.

Psalm 40
2　He brought me up also out of an horrible pit, out of the miry clay, and set my feet upon a rock, and established my goings.

_____

_____

_____

_____

_____

Just as God has a determined destination for you, He also has a path for you to follow to get there.
Listen closely to the Holy Spirit as he guides you in the direction of God's purpose.

Destiny & Purpose

Everyone will die, but not everyone will live.

1 Thessalonians 3
[8] For now we live, if ye stand fast in the Lord.

_____

_____

_____

_____

_____

To live is not to merely have been born and to have died. It is, on the contrary, to be born again, die of the flesh, and lead others to God so that they, too, would be born again.

Destiny & Purpose

When God speaks to you, He does so from where you are going – not from where you are.

Jeremiah 29

[10] For thus saith the LORD, That after seventy years be accomplished at Babylon I will visit you, and perform my good word toward you, in causing you to return to this place. [11] For I know the thoughts that I think toward you, saith the LORD, thoughts of peace, and not of evil, to give you an expected end.

Our all-knowing, all-powerful God not only sees where you are, but He already knows where you will end up. He will often give what seems to be illogical instructions because He is fully aware of what is coming your way. Isn't it comforting to know that He is in control?

Destiny & Purpose

The dog may bark, but the train rolls on.

Ecclesiastes 6

¹⁰ That which hath been is named already, and it is known that it is man: neither may he contend with him that is mightier than he.

_____

_____

_____

_____

_____

Your future will come to past whether you are prepared or not!

Your Mouth: Your greatest tool or weapon

Your words are containers for power.

Proverbs 18

21 Death and life are in the power of the tongue: and they that love it shall eat the fruit thereof.

_____

_____

_____

_____

_____

Your tongue can be your most powerful weapon, or your greatest tool.
Choose today to speak only positive things over yourself and others.

Your Mouth: Your greatest tool or weapon

What lives in your mouth – it's not long before it lives in your life.

Job 15

[5] For your iniquity teaches your mouth, and you choose the tongue of the crafty.

_____

_____

_____

_____

_____

You have the ability to speak things into existence in your own life.
What have you been repeating lately? Ask the Lord to guard your tongue as
you become more careful about the blessings you bestow by your mouth.

Your Mouth: Your greatest tool or weapon

Every man has a king and a fool in him – the one you talk to responds.

Proverbs 15

[1] A soft answer turneth away wrath: but grievous words stir up anger.

_____

_____

_____

_____

_____

Everyone has weakness and greatness.
Your words have the ability to pull either of those out of a person.

Your Mouth: Your greatest tool or weapon

He who is good at making excuses is seldom good
at anything else.

Exodus 4
[10] And Moses said unto the LORD, O my LORD, I am not eloquent, neither
heretofore, nor since thou hast spoken unto thy servant: but I am slow of speech, and
of a slow tongue.

_____

_____

_____

_____

_____

*Your stutter won't stop your anointing! Stop thinking of reasons why you can't step out
and complete the work that God began in you.
Making excuses only convinces yourself and others that you cannot do it!*

Your Mouth: Your greatest tool or weapon

If you want to know how you think, listen to your mouth.

Job 15

6 Your own mouth condemns you, and not I; yes, your own lips testify against you.

_____

_____

_____

_____

_____

Have you ever let an insult "slip" out? If your mouth tends to be critical, you may have a heart issue with being judgmental. Ask God to show you those things in your heart that are not of Him, so that you can purge them before you hurt someone.

Your Mouth: Your greatest tool or weapon

Mountains don't move unless you speak to them.

Mark 11

[23] For verily I say unto you, That whosoever shall say unto this mountain, Be thou removed, and be thou cast into the sea; and shall not doubt in his heart, but shall believe that those things which he saith shall come to pass; he shall have whatsoever he saith.

_____

_____

_____

_____

_____

The bible tells us that whatever we speak in faith will come to pass. Try God today by exercising the power of faith with the power of your words, and see Him move mountains for you!

Your Mouth: Your greatest tool or weapon

Speaking comes from the ability to hear.

Matthew 13
[43] …Who hath ears to hear, let him hear.

_____

_____

_____

_____

_____

Your ability to control your tongue will stem from your ability to listen to the direction of the Holy Spirit. He will always caution you to guard your words so that they will not offend others..

Your Mouth: Your greatest tool or weapon

Don't say anything in your winter that will hurt you in your springtime.

Proverbs 18

7   A fool's mouth is his destruction, and his lips are the snare of his soul.

_____

_____

_____

_____

_____

Once you have released words, you can never take them back. The only way to ensure that you never regret what you say is to be careful to think before you speak and speak with love, no matter how you feel.

Your Mouth: Your greatest tool or weapon

It seems like God is limited –
He will do nothing until someone asks.

John 11

[22] But I know, that even now, whatsoever thou wilt ask of God, God will give it thee.

_____

_____

_____

_____

_____

God will not move until we ask, but once we ask, His power is unlimited! Are you holding
God back by refusing to ask for something? Talk to Him today. He's waiting to bless you!

Your Mouth: Your greatest tool or weapon

You frame your world by the words you speak.

Romans 4

[17] (As it is written, I have made thee a father of many nations,) before him whom he believed, even God, who quickeneth the dead, and calleth those things which be not as though they were.

_____

_____

_____

_____

_____

God called things that were not as though they were, and they came to be! As children of God, we have that same privilege. Exercise your right to bring blessings into your life today by speaking them!

Your Mouth: Your greatest tool or weapon

God cannot do more for you than your words allow Him to do.

Matthew 13

[58]   And he did not many mighty works there because of their unbelief.

_____

_____

_____

_____

_____

Are you limiting God by speaking words of doubt about a situation? Rectify that now by
speaking words of blessing and abundance over your life from this point forward.

Your Mouth: Your greatest tool or weapon

Silence cannot be misquoted.

Proverbs 17

27 He that hath knowledge spareth his words: and a man of understanding
is of an excellent spirit.

_____

_____

_____

_____

_____

Verbal arguments should not be an issue if you learn to be disciplined in your speech. Allow God to fight your battles for you by giving the situation over to Him and submitting to His will.

Your Mouth: Your greatest tool or weapon

Your heart is a filter that pollutes or purifies your words.

Matthew 12(b)

[34] . . . for out of the abundance of the heart the mouth speaketh.

_____

_____

_____

_____

_____

*Just as your heart is exposed by the words that you say, your heart can also be used as a gauge of the
Holy Spirit to know when you should or should not partake in certain conversations.
Exercise wisdom and discernment by following your heart's directions.*

Your Mouth: Your greatest tool or weapon

Start making your words line up with His words.

Ephesians 4

[29] Let no corrupt communication proceed out of your mouth, but that which is good
to the use of edifying, that it may minister grace unto the hearers.

_____

_____

_____

_____

_____

The bible says that you are snared by the words of your own mouth. Everyday,
wake up and speak spirit-filled life words over yourself, as the Bible declares to
"rejoice and be glad" in each new day God makes.

Mindset

You speak outwardly what you hear inwardly.

Genesis 6

5 And God saw that the wickedness of man was great in the earth, and that every imagination of the thoughts of his heart was only evil continually.

_____

_____

_____

_____

_____

Experts say if you have a negative thought and it is attached to a feeling, you tend to repeat that thought subconsciously 600 times a day. Purpose in your heart to think only on things of God so that negativity does not have the chance to inhabit your speech.

Mindset

Your life will ultimately take on the direction of your thinking.

Proverbs 23
[7] For as he thinketh in his heart, so is he...

_____

_____

_____

_____

_____

Thoughts of worry and doubt can be as damaging to you as words of worry and doubt.
Make a conscious effort to change your thoughts to expectation and anticipation of what
God is going to do in your life.

Mindset

Everything tangible started in someone's mind/thoughts.

1 Chronicles 28

[11] Then David gave his son Solomon the plans for the portico of the temple, its buildings, its storerooms, its upper parts, its inner rooms and the place of atonement. [12] He gave him the plans of all that the Spirit had put in his mind for the courts of the temple of the LORD and all the surrounding rooms, for the treasuries of the temple of God and for the treasuries for the dedicated things.

_____

_____

_____

_____

_____

All achievement and all earthly riches have their beginnings in an idea or dream.

Mindset

(Thomas Edison): "Many think I'm smarter – I'm not – Other men think of many things all day – I think of one thing."

Isaiah 26
3 Thou wilt keep him in perfect peace, whose mind is stayed on thee: because he trusteth in thee.

_____

_____

_____

_____

_____

1 Chronicles 28
9 *...for the LORD searcheth all hearts, and understandeth all the imaginations of the thoughts: if thou seek him, he will be found of thee; but if thou forsake him, he will cast thee off for ever*

Mindset

Nothing big ever comes from thinking small.

1 Corinthians 2

[16] For who hath known the mind of the Lord, that he may instruct him?
but we have the mind of Christ.

_____

_____

_____

_____

_____

If you have the mind of Christ, how can you place limitations on yourself by not using
His creativity and insights to imagine a better you, and better situation, and a better future?

Mindset

Only hungry minds can grow.

Matthew 5

6 Blessed are they which do hunger and thirst after righteousness:
for they shall be filled.

_____

_____

_____

_____

_____

*Seek God and the peace of mind that only He can provide, and you'll be amazed by the
awesome clarity you will have to see your way out of anything.*

Mindset

The only access the devil has to you is through your mind.

Philippians 4

[8] Finally, brethren, whatsoever things are true, whatsoever things are honest, whatsoever things are just, whatsoever things are pure, whatsoever things are lovely, whatsoever things are of good report; if there be any virtue, and if there be any praise, think on these things.

_____

_____

_____

_____

_____

Have you opened a door to the enemy by allowing him to cloud your mind with doubt and negativity?
Make a decision to think only on the things of God, and see how situations turn around today!

Mindset

Your only boundaries in life are your own perception of potential.

Genesis 11

[6] … and now nothing will be restrained from them, which they have imagined to do.

_____

_____

_____

_____

_____

What are you imagining for yourself? If it's not peace, increase, and spiritual growth, THINK AGAIN! Don't be your own enemy by refusing to accept the limitless potential of You with God's help.

Mindset

Creativity begins in the thought life.

2 Corinthians 10

[5] Casting down imaginations, and every high thing that exalteth itself against the knowledge of God, and bringing into captivity every thought to the obedience of Christ

_____

_____

_____

_____

_____

We are not instructed to quit imagining, but to destroy every imagination or thought that are contrary to God's and His will for our life.

Mindset

Attitude is a little thing that makes a big difference.

Philippians 2

5 Let this mind be in you, which was also in Christ Jesus:

6 Who, being in the form of God, thought it not robbery to be equal with God:

7 But made himself of no reputation, and took upon him the form of a servant, and was made in the likeness of men:

8 And being found in fashion as a man, he humbled himself, and became obedient unto death, even the death of the cross.

If you have the mind of Christ, you also have the meek, and humble attitude of a servant.
Tap into that attitude today as you submit not only to God's will, but also to
that of anyone in authority over you.

Mindset

Thoughts become Words → Action → Habit → Character → Destiny.

Psalm 19
[14] Let the words of my mouth, and the meditation of my heart, be acceptable in thy sight, O LORD, my strength, and my redeemer.

_____

_____

_____

_____

_____

Everything in your world originates in your thoughts. What type of life have you allowed your thoughts to paint for you?

Mindset

If your thoughts, philosophies, ideas or reasonings are
built on anything but the Word of God,
they are nothing but sinking sand.

Romans 12

2 And be not conformed to this world: but be ye transformed by the renewing of your
mind, that ye may prove what is that good, and acceptable, and perfect, will of God.

_____

_____

_____

_____

_____

*Yield to God today, asking Him to renew your mind so that you will no longer be a hindrance to
yourself in pursuing all that He has for you.*

Mindset

Focus determines mastery.

Proverbs 16

3 Commit thy works unto the LORD, and thy thoughts shall be established.

_____

_____

_____

_____

_____

If it can keep your attention, it has mastered you. What have you spent too much time thinking about?
Bills? Illness? Focus your works on God, and He will direct your thoughts to Him, as well.

Mindset

Perception is more powerful than reality.

1 Corinthians 2

⁹ But as it is written, Eye hath not seen, nor ear heard, neither have entered into the heart of man, the things which God hath prepared for them that love him.

¹⁰ But God hath revealed them unto us by his Spirit: for the Spirit searcheth all things, yea, the deep things of God.

_____

_____

_____

_____

_____

God speaks to you from someplace in your future, where things look a lot different from your present situation. Your ability to see and believe in that revelation more than your current situation is what will drive you into your destiny.

Mentorship or Being an Example

People need believable heroes.

Philippians 3

[17] Brethren, be followers together of me, and mark them which walk so as ye have us for an ensample.

_____

_____

_____

_____

_____

The greatest hero you can ever have is Jesus. Set Him as the ultimate example to live your life by, instead of a fallible man.

Mentorship or Being an Example

You learn from mentors or experience.

Deuteronomy 32

[11] As an eagle stirreth up her nest, fluttereth over her young, spreadeth abroad her wings, taketh them, beareth them on her wings:

_____

_____

_____

_____

_____

The mother eagle coaches her young while in the nest, but she also takes them out to fly and experience life for themselves. True learning in life will come in either of these two methods.

Mentorship or Being an Example

Parasites want what you earned.
Protégés want what you learned.

Luke 6
40 A pupil is not superior to his teacher, but everyone [when he is] completely trained
(readjusted, restored, set to rights, and perfected) will be like his teacher.

_____

_____

_____

_____

_____

*A Protégé, your heart's desire is to be like your mentor. His desire for you is to be even better than he
is. When you find yourself seeking what your mentor has, instead of what he can teach you, seek God
to make your motives pure.*

Mentorship or Being an Example

We need an instructed people if we are to have
a fruitful people.

Isaiah 33

6 And wisdom and knowledge shall be the stability of thy times, and strength of
salvation: the fear of the LORD is his treasure.

_____

_____

_____

_____

_____

You cannot bear fruit if you do not know how to nurture the seeds within yourself.
Seek God for wisdom, and seek mentors and experience for head knowledge.

Mentorship or Being an Example

Motivation is deeper than words.

Isaiah 32
[8] But the noble man makes noble plans, and by noble deeds he stands.

_____

_____

_____

_____

_____

*Motives have a lot to do with who you are. It does not matter what you say or do,
if you have wrong motives, it is all for naught. Seek God to perform a personal
inventory of your motives in every situation.*

Treasure of the Day   *Paula White*

Mentorship or Being an Example

You will influence others only to the portion you are
willing to sacrifice yourself.

1 John 3

16 Hereby perceive we the love of God, because he laid down his life for us:
and we ought to lay down our lives for the brethren.

_____

_____

_____

_____

_____

*God is the ultimate influence in your lives because He loved us enough to give His life for us. What are
you willing to give to those you are mentoring? By his example, we should be willing to lay down our
lives (our priorities, our time, our strength) as well.*

Mentorship or Being an Example

The teacher has not taught until the pupil has learned.

Deuteronomy 4

[5] Behold, I have taught you statutes and judgments, even as the LORD my God commanded me, that ye should do so in the land whither ye go to possess it.
[6] Keep therefore and do them; for this is your wisdom and your understanding in the sight of the nations, which shall hear all these statutes, and say, Surely this great nation is a wise and understanding people.

_____

_____

_____

_____

_____

Teaching others for your own sake does nothing for the development of others.
Until those you lead can also be called leaders, your work is not done.

Mentorship or Being an Example

Your legacy outlives you.

Psalm 102

[18] This shall be written for the generation to come: and the people which shall be created shall praise the LORD.

_____

_____

_____

_____

What type of legacy are you leaving behind? Is it debt? Negativity? Hopelessness?
The effect you have today will touch others for generations to come.

Mentorship or Being an Example

Your mentor is not your friend, but your coach.

John 8

12   Then spake Jesus again unto them, saying, I am the light of the world: he that followeth me shall not walk in darkness, but shall have the light of life.

_____

_____

_____

_____

_____

Jesus did not say, he that "hangs out with me" shall not walk in darkness. True teaching occurs when the teacher and the student can separate their personal feelings from the lesson at hand.

Mentorship or Being an Example

You cannot take someone where you have never been.

1 Corinthians 11
[1]   Be ye followers of me, even as I also am of Christ.

_____

_____

_____

_____

_____

This statement by Paul should be an example to each us of as we choose mentors. Who have they followed, and where have they been? That will tell you where they can take you.

Mentorship or Being an Example

A leader does not imitate but rather creates.

Genesis 1

[27] So God created man in his own image, in the image of God created he him; male and female created he them.

_____

_____

_____

_____

_____

If God created us in His image, and He is the creator of all things, we, too have the ability to create. Celebrate the supreme uniqueness of YOU, and lead others to appreciate their own uniqueness as well.

Mentorship or Being an Example

No one wakes up polished – you must be developed.

1 Peter 2

[2] Like newborn babies you should crave (thirst for, earnestly desire) the pure (unadulterated) spiritual milk, that by it you may be nurtured and grow unto [completed] salvation (AMP).

_____

_____

_____

_____

_____

In order to mature and grow, we must undergo learning processes. In fact, your entire life should be considered one long learning process, as you seek to perfect your walk with Christ.

Mentorship or Being an Example

What enters your life determines what will exit.

Proverbs 13
20 He that walketh with wise men shall be wise:
but a companion of fools shall be destroyed.

_____

_____

_____

_____

_____

*Influence is critical when you are in the early stages of learning and growing. Know that you will take
on the likeness and character of whatever you are around while you are developing.*

Mentorship or Being an Example

Mentors are your gate to greatness and your bridge to blessings.

Proverbs 15

22 Without counsel purposes are disappointed: but in the multitude of counsellors they are established.

_____

_____

_____

_____

_____

Mentors should serve as your very own Board of Directors in life. Seek wisdom and counsel from a solid circle of people you trust, respect, and admire.

Adversity

You can reverse a curse through God's power.

Jeremiah 26

[13] Therefore now amend your ways and your doings and obey the voice of the Lord your God; then the Lord will relent and reverse the decision concerning the evil which He has pronounced against you.

_____

_____

_____

_____

_____

No matter the situation, God can step in and turn it around for you. Rely on Him to be the mighty Savior that he wants to be in your life.

Treasure of the Day   Paula White

For every blessing there is testing
– for every opportunity there is adversity.

Job 23
[10] But he knoweth the way that I take: when he hath tried me,
I shall come forth as gold.

_____

_____

_____

_____

_____

Thank God that trouble is knocking at your door! That means opportunity and blessings are right around the corner. Allow this adversity to heat you up and remove impurities so that, in the need, you can come forth as pure gold.

Adversity

Use the rocks people throw at you – use them to build your life – use them to build a wall around you.

2 Corinthians 12

10 Therefore I take pleasure in infirmities, in reproaches, in necessities, in persecutions, in distresses for Christ's sake: for when I am weak, then am I strong.

_____

_____

_____

_____

_____

Adversity is not a personal attack against you, but against your mission in life.
Use your persecutions to build yourself up to be stronger in the fight for righteousness.

Treasure of the Day

Paula White

Adversity

Your stumbling block is going to be your stepping-stone.

Genesis 14
[20] And blessed, praised, and glorified be God Most High, Who has given your foes into your hand! (AMP)

_____

_____

_____

_____

_____

Once you give the situation over to God, He will work it out in ways that you may have never expected. He can change the heart of any man. Those who you have considered your foes may come back again as your biggest supporters.

Adversity

You don't conquer without conflict…
You don't win without war.

1 Corinthians 11
[19] No doubt there have to be differences among you to show
which of you have God's approval.

_____

_____

_____

_____

_____

People will always come against you – no matter who you are.
The beauty of it is that God uses conflicts to show You who you are.

Adversity

God allows us to intrude on a private dialogue
between a mess and a message.

Job 36
[15] He delivers the afflicted in their affliction and opens their ears [to His voice] in
adversity.

_____

_____

_____

_____

_____

*Take a moment to remove yourself from your situation and listen to what God is saying to you in the
midst of it all. It could be that your answer lies right where you are – and you had to get here to hear it.*

New levels mean new devils.

1 Peter 5

8 Be self-controlled and alert. Your enemy the devil prowls around like a roaring lion looking for someone to devour.

9 Resist him, standing firm in the faith, because you know that your brothers throughout the world are undergoing the same kind of sufferings. (NIV)

When you are promoted to new levels (spiritually, professionally, financially, etc.), you move closer to your divine destiny. Seeing this, the enemy stages greater attacks to distract you from what God has planned for you. Resist him, and he will flee.

Adversity

You can disagree agreeably.

Matthew 5

[25] Agree with thine adversary quickly, whiles thou art in the way with him; lest at any time the adversary deliver thee to the judge, and the judge deliver thee to the officer, and thou be cast into prison.

Disagreements have a way of growing way out of proportion and propelling into deep-rooted animosity. Neuter your disagreements quickly by getting to the root of the problem and talking it out in a Christian manner until all parties are comfortable.

Adversity

Some of the people who fight you are preparing you for where you're going.

2 Corinthians 4

[17] For our light affliction, which is but for a moment, worketh for us a far more exceeding and eternal weight of glory;

_____

_____

_____

_____

_____

Sometimes, the people who come against you in life, are "pop quizzes" for an exam that you will have later in life. Get through this "light thing" now, so that God can promote you to do the real work He has planned for you.

Adversity

If people can shut you up, then they can shut you down.

2 Timothy 1

[8] Be not thou therefore ashamed of the testimony of our Lord,
nor of me his prisoner: but be thou partaker of the afflictions
of the gospel according to the power of God;

_____

_____

_____

_____

_____

Don't let anyone stop your testimony. If someone can stop you from testifying about the goodness of God, they can stop you from believing in it.

Adversity

When you can't forgive, try surrendering.

Psalm 86

5　For thou, Lord, art good, and ready to forgive; and plenteous in mercy
unto all them that call upon thee.

---

*Yield yourself to God and ask him to place forgiveness in your heart.
Call upon Him and He will hear.*

The door of opportunity swings on the hinges of opposition.

1 Corinthians 16
[9] For a wide door of opportunity for effectual [service] has opened to me [there, a great and promising one], and [there are] many adversaries. (AMP)

Adversity is a natural occurrence in life in that it almost always precedes breakthrough. You should begin to worry if there is never any adversity!

Adversity

You cannot control circumstances, but you can control your response.

Matthew 5

11 Blessed are ye, when men shall revile you, and persecute you, and shall say all manner of evil against you falsely, for my sake.

12 Rejoice, and be exceeding glad: for great is your reward in heaven: for so persecuted they the prophets which were before you.

_____

_____

_____

_____

_____

Follow the example of the prophets and Jesus by taking all insults with a grain of sand.
The wrong response to persecution could delay your destiny..

Adversity

When you get out of the boat and start walking on water,
get ready for all hell to break out.

Luke 6

[22] Blessed are ye, when men shall hate you, and when they shall separate you
from their company, and shall reproach you, and cast out your name as evil,
for the Son of man's sake.

[23] Rejoice ye in that day, and leap for joy: for, behold, your reward is great in heaven:
for in the like manner did their fathers unto the prophets.

_____

_____

_____

_____

_____

When you begin to step out on faith, your critics have to justify why they are still sitting in the boat.
It's easier to criticize you than to walk on water.

Affiliations

You become a product of what you are around.

1 Corinthians 15

[33] Do not be so deceived and misled! Evil companionships (communion, associations) corrupt and deprave good manners and morals and character. (AMP)

_____

_____

_____

_____

_____

Don't be misled to think that you can be an influence to others, without them rubbing off on you. Protect your anointing by surrounding yourself with people who have purpose and are seeking growth in the same ways that you are.

Affiliations

Don't nurture what needs to be neutered in your life.

Lamentations 1

2 She weepeth sore in the night, and her tears are on her cheeks: among all her lovers she hath none to comfort her: all her friends have dealt treacherously with her, they are become her enemies.

_____

_____

_____

_____

_____

Cut off bad affiliations today. Don't allow them to drain you of your joy or your anointing.

Affiliations

People either (+) add, (-) subtract, (x) multiply or
(/) divide in your life.

Psalm 1

¹ Blessed is the man that walketh not in the counsel of the ungodly,
nor standeth in the way of sinners, nor sitteth in the seat of the scornful.

_____

_____

_____

_____

_____

While pouring into others is good, don't surround yourself only with those who take from you.
In order to effectively give, you must be poured into, as well.

Affiliations

Friends create comfort for you.
Enemies create rewards and challenges.

Proverbs 27

[6] Faithful are the wounds of a friend; but the kisses of an enemy are deceitful.

_____

_____

_____

_____

_____

Friends and enemies serve very different, yet very important, purposes in your life.
Allow your friends to build you up. Use your enemies to show you those things
within yourself that are your strengths and gifts.

Affiliations

The associations in your life show me your value system.

1 Corinthians 10
[33] Just as I myself strive to please [to accommodate myself to the opinions, desires, and interests of others, adapting myself to] all men in everything I do, not aiming at or considering my own profit and advantage, but that of the many in order that they may be saved. (AMP)

----

*If you find yourself fellowshipping only with the unsaved, make sure your motive is
to shed light into darkness by spreading the gospel to them.
Otherwise, your walk may be compromised by their influence on you.*

Affiliations

Anyone who will sin with you will eventually sin against you.

Psalm 50

[18] When you see a thief, you associate with him, and you have taken part with adulterers. (AMP)

_____

_____

_____

_____

_____

Don't be deceived. One who steals with you, will steal from you. One who gossips with you will gossip about you. Anyone who is not helping you in your walk, may be hindering you.

Affiliations

A true friend sees beyond what you are to what you can be.

Judges 6

[12] And the Angel of the Lord appeared unto him, and said unto him, the LORD is with the, thou mighty man of valor.

_____

_____

_____

_____

_____

Just as God sees you and speaks to you in your future state, a true friend should be able to see beyond your current condition to the awesome potential of who you are called to be.

Affiliations

Who you are around helps determine where you are going to go.

John 19

[25] Now there stood by the cross of Jesus his mother, and his mother's sister, Mary, the wife of Cleaphas, and Mary Magdalene.

_____

_____

_____

_____

_____

Even Mary Magdalene was able to change her situation by changing her environment.
She began to surround herself with mighty women of God, and soon she became one as well.

Affiliations

Don't be so guarded that you build a wall that imprisons you.

Proverbs 18
24 A man that hath friends must shew himself friendly: and there is a
friend that sticketh closer than a brother.

_____

_____

_____

_____

_____

*For others to consider you to be friendly, you must be approachable and warm-hearted. You do the world
a disservice when you don't allow others the opportunity to get to know the incredible person you are.*

Affiliations

Go where you are celebrated and not tolerated.

Amos 3
3 Can two walk together, except they be agreed?

You cannot be appreciated where there is strife and disagreement. Surround yourself
with those who know who you are in Christ and celebrate that with you.

Affiliations

Never complain about what you tolerate.
Behavior permitted is behavior accepted.

2 Corinthians 6
14 Be ye not unequally yoked together with unbelievers: for what fellowship hath
righteousness with unrighteousness? and what communion hath light with darkness?

_____

_____

_____

_____

_____

*If you remain in an environment of sin, you have no right to complain about what
takes place in that environment. Your presence equates to tolerance.*

Affiliations

You must eliminate the noise in your life to hear effectively.

Jeremiah 46

[17] They cried there, Pharaoh king of Egypt is destroyed and is only a noise; he has let the appointed time [in which God had him on probation] pass by! (AMP)

_____

_____

_____

_____

_____

Pharaoh was disregarded and considered to be just a loud noise because he was out of covenant with God. Be sure to mute all of the "noise" in your life that may be hindering you from hearing the Word of God.

Affiliations

There is success by association.

Genesis 30

27 And Laban said unto him, I pray thee, if I have found favor in thine eyes, tarry: for I have learned by experience that the LORD hath blessed me for thy sake.

_____

_____

_____

_____

_____

Some of the blessings in your life are because of who you are around.

Affiliations

Staff your weaknesses.

Ephesians 4

[11] And he gave some, apostles; and some, prophets; and some, evangelists; and some, pastors and teachers;

[12] For the perfecting of the saints, for the work of the ministry, for the edifying of the body of Christ:

[13] Till we all come in the unity of the faith, and of the knowledge of the Son of God, unto a perfect man, unto the measure of the stature of the fulness of Christ:

_____

_____

_____

_____

_____

Every person has unique gifts that can be used for the body of Christ. If you have a weakness in an area, build your staff with people who are strong in that area to create balance, and ensure that everyone flows with their gifts.

Falling Down

Fail your way to success.

1 Kings 8

[33] When thy people Israel be smitten down before the enemy, because they have sinned against thee, and shall turn again to thee, and confess thy name, and pray, and make supplication unto thee in this house:

[34] Then hear thou in heaven, and forgive the sin of thy people Israel, and bring them again unto the land which thou gavest unto their fathers.

_____

_____

_____

_____

_____

The road to success is a very bumpy one, filled with mistakes and mishaps. The only way to reach your destination is through the obstacles – but once you get there you'll appreciate the journey all the more!

Falling Down

Failure is not falling down – but staying down.

2 Chronicles 15
[7] Be ye strong therefore, and let not your hands be weak: for your work shall be rewarded.

_____

_____

_____

_____

_____

Don't be discouraged by the mistakes you have made.
Wallowing in guilt and shame will only delay your destiny.

Falling Down

Failure is part of learning.

Romans 5
³ And not only so, but we glory in tribulations also:
knowing that tribulation worketh patience;

_____

_____

_____

_____

_____

Every time you fall, you move a little closer to the goal because you learn what not to do to get there.
It's better to have tried and failed than never to have tried.

Falling Down

The call was before the fall.

Isaiah 41

[4] Who hath wrought and done it, calling the generations from the beginning? I the LORD, the first, and with the last; I am he.

_____

_____

_____

_____

_____

God planted a seed of destiny in you in the beginning of time.
Your failure has not changed what you are destined to achieve in life.

Falling Down

Only those who risk going too far will ever know
how far they can go.

Philippians 2

[29] Receive him therefore in the Lord with all gladness, and hold such men in esteem;
[30] because for the work of Christ he came close to death, not regarding his life, to
supply what was lacking in your service toward me.

_____

_____

_____

_____

_____

Timothy risked his life for the gospel. What will you risk to see what God has in store for you?

Falling Down

Don't confuse your mistakes with your value as a person.

Proverbs 24

[15] Lay not wait, O wicked man, against the dwelling of the righteous; spoil not his resting place:

[16] For a just man falleth seven times, and riseth up again: but the wicked shall fall into mischief.

_____

_____

_____

_____

_____

The real value of you is displayed when you get up from falling.
Decide today to finish the race with your head held high.

Falling Down

You might be disappointed if you fail, but you
are doomed if you never try.

2 Chronicles 31

[21] And in every work that he began in the service of the house of God, in the law and
in the commandment, to seek his God, he did it with all his heart. So he prospered.
(NKJV)

_____

_____

_____

_____

_____

Stand firm and persevere knowing that God will reward your pure heart and desire to serve Him.

Falling Down

The more you walk with God, the less He tells you what to do.
He expects you to act on what you already know.

Colossians 2

6 As ye have therefore received Christ Jesus the Lord, so walk ye in him:
7 Rooted and built up in him, and stablished in the faith, as ye have been taught,
abounding therein with thanksgiving.

_____

_____

_____

_____

_____

God trusts you to obey His will and act on what you have learned about Him.
Not hearing from Him is no excuse to move away from Him.

Falling Down

What you had for a long time can depart from you in a short time.

James 4

14 Whereas ye know not what shall be on the morrow. For what is your life? It is even a vapour, that appeareth for a little time, and then vanisheth away.

_____

_____

_____

_____

_____

Put your trust in God and things of the spirit that will last for eternity. All else will fade away in time.

Falling Down

Mistakes are often your best educator.

Psalm 119

71 It is good for me that I have been afflicted; that I might learn thy statutes.

_____

_____

_____

_____

_____

Take the time to evaluate your mistakes to see what you can learn from them.
Apply that learning to your life so that you will not make the same mistakes again.

Falling Down

Delay does not mean denial.

Hebrews 6

[15] And so, after he had patiently endured, he obtained the promise.

_____

_____

_____

_____

_____

*Don't be discouraged by a delay. Take the time to reflect on how far you've come,
and revel in the awesome reward of the end.*

Falling Down

God does not release you from your purpose
when you make a decision in your flesh.

Jeremiah 8

⁴ Moreover thou shalt say unto them, Thus saith the LORD; Shall they fall, and not
arise? shall he turn away, and not return?

_____

_____

_____

_____

_____

*Acting in the flesh is a temporary setback, but you should not allow it to distract you
from staying your course. Repent, forgive yourself and keep going.*

Falling Down

As long as you don't quit, you will never lose.

Mark 13

13 And ye shall be hated of all men for my name's sake: but he that shall endure unto the end, the same shall be saved.

_____

_____

_____

_____

_____

The only way to succeed is to keep going. God's Word tells us to endure to the end to see the fullness of His promise. He will sustain you until the end.

Falling Down

The only reason people fail is broken focus.

Philippians 3

[13] No, dear brothers and sisters, I am still not all I should be, but I am focusing all my energies on this one thing: Forgetting the past and looking forward to what lies ahead.
(AMP)

Obstacles are what you see when you take your eyes off the goal. Purpose in your heart to ignore your obstacles, and focus only on the destiny that God has called you to.

Change

Only a fool repeats the same thing and expects
a different result.

Proverbs 26
[11] As a dog returneth to his vomit, so a fool returneth to his folly.

----

*Mistakes are opportunities to learn what NOT to do. How can you ever succeed if
you continue doing the very thing that has delayed your destiny?*

Change

God transforms me with His truths.

Romans 12

[2] And be not conformed to this world: but be ye transformed by the renewing of your mind, that ye may prove what is that good, and acceptable, and perfect, will of God.

_____

_____

_____

_____

_____

The only way to mke a significant and lasting change is to ask God to transform you. Study His word to know who He has called you to be, and ask Him to help you become that person.

Change

The person who never changes his opinion never corrects his mistakes.

Luke 5

36 And he spake also a parable unto them; No man putteth a piece of a new garment upon an old; if otherwise, then both the new maketh a rent, and the piece that was taken out of the new agreeth not with the old.

37 And no man putteth new wine into old bottles; else the new wine will burst the bottles, and be spilled, and the bottles shall perish.

38 But new wine must be put into new bottles; and both are preserved.

39 No man also having drunk old wine straightway desireth new: for he saith, The old is better.

_____

_____

_____

_____

_____

Change is necessary for all of us to grow into who we are called to be.
Your ability to be flexible is an important factor in how much you can change.

Change

You cannot be successful and sensitive.

1 Samuel 1

⁶ And her adversary also provoked her sore, for to make her fret,
because the LORD had shut up her womb.

_____

_____

_____

_____

_____

To achieve and maintain true success, you must develop thick skin while maintaining a tender heart.

Change

Often "old friends" don't understand the "new change" in you.

2 Corinthians 5

17 Therefore if any man be in Christ, he is a new creature:
old things are passed away; behold, all things are become new.

_____

_____

_____

_____

_____

*Many people won't be able to appreciate the changes you will undergo as you move into
who God wants you to be. Be patient with them, but also be wise enough to know when they
become more of a liability than an asset.*

Change

You must give people a chance to transition their life.

Isaiah 40

7 The grass withereth, the flower fadeth: because the spirit of the LORD bloweth
upon it: surely the people is grass.

8 The grass withereth, the flower fadeth: but the word of our God shall stand for ever.

---

*Just as you expect others to be patient and understand your transition, you also owe that to people
around you. Some people will take longer than others to come to Christ, but it is your patience and love
that will attract them to what He has to offer.*

Change

God loves you too much to leave you the same.

2 Corinthians 7

9 Yet I am glad now, not because you were pained, but because you were pained into repentance [and so turned back to God]; for you felt a grief such as God meant you to feel, so that in nothing you might suffer loss through us or harm for what we did.

(AMP)

_____

_____

_____

_____

_____

*Find comfort in knowing that God is only applying pressure to mold you into
the person He already knows you can be.*

Change

When you always use an excuse, you give
up the power to change.

Ephesians 5

6 Let no one delude and deceive you with empty excuses and groundless arguments
[for these sins], for through these things the wrath of God comes upon the sons of
rebellion and disobedience. (AMP)

_____

_____

_____

_____

_____

Excuses are useless tools that allow you to stay stagnant.
Make the decision today to move out of the "land of excuses" and into the "land of excellence!"

Change

The key to transformation is to walk in the spirit and not the flesh.

Ezekiel 36

[27] And I will put my Spirit within you and cause you to walk in My statutes, and you shall heed My ordinances and do them.

Your natural mind may be hindering you from spiritual growth.
Begin to seek direction from the Holy Spirit and watch God transform you!

Change

Everything that grows changes.

1 Corinthians 13

[11] When I was a child, I spake as a child, I understood as a child, I thought as a child: but when I became a man, I put away childish things.

_____

_____

_____

_____

_____

Change is necessary for growth. Nothing that is alive can grow without changing form in some way. Being open to change means being open to growth.

You can't change what you don't acknowledge.

2 Chronicles 7

[14] If my people, which are called by my name, shall humble themselves, and pray, and seek my face, and turn from their wicked ways; then will I hear from heaven, and will forgive their sin, and will heal their land.

_____

_____

_____

_____

_____

The first step in changing is asking the Holy Spirit to reveal to you those areas that require an adjustment. Once that is clear, you will be able to make deliberate changes in the right areas.

Change

Anytime there is change – there is opportunity.

1 John 2

[8] Yet I am writing you a new commandment, which is true (is realized) in Him and in you, because the darkness (moral blindness) is clearing away and the true Light (the revelation of God in Christ) is already shining. (AMP)

_____

_____

_____

_____

_____

Change is good! Don't be afraid to experience something new or different. Expanding your horizons allows you to see the world from a viewpoint other than your own.

Change

Inward power has the ability to transform outward conditions.

Romans 15

13 Now the God of hope fill you with all joy and peace in believing, that ye may abound in hope, through the power of the Holy Ghost.

_____

_____

_____

_____

_____

The Holy Spirit residing inside of you gives you the spiritual fortitude that your flesh needs to change and grow into the person that God has called you to be.

Change

Mediocrity gets no attention.

2 Corinthians 5
[20] Now then we are ambassadors for Christ…

_____

_____

_____

_____

_____

Why settle for just enough? God is the God of more than enough.
He is calling you to expect more of yourself because you are in the world to represent Him.

Balance & Taking Care of Yourself

Weariness is to lose the sense of pleasure.

Ecclesiastes 4

[1] THEN I returned and considered all the oppressions that are practiced under the sun: And I beheld the tears of the oppressed, and they had no comforter; and on the side of their oppressors was power, but they [too] had no comforter.
[2] So I praised and thought more fortunate those who have been long dead than the living, who are still alive. (AMP)

_____

_____

_____

_____

_____

When you lose the ability to appreciate and enjoy anything, you lose your lust for life. Don't allow anything to steal your joy, the joy that God has placed in you.

Balance & Taking Care of Yourself

Overloaded people fail.

Psalm 6

7 My eye grows dim because of grief; it grows old because of all my enemies.

_____

_____

_____

_____

_____

Be careful to manage your workload. Success is only possible if you have the time and energy to devote to finishing tasks!

Balance & Taking Care of Yourself

The question is not <u>how long</u> we live but <u>how well</u> we live.
What matters are the moments we live life to the fullest.

Ecclesiastes 5
[20] For he shall not much remember [seriously] the days of his life, because God [Himself] answers and corresponds to the joy of his heart [the tranquillity of God is mirrored in him]. (AMP)

_____

_____

_____

_____

_____

*It doesn't matter if you live to be 100 if you don't have any good memories to reflect on.
Take the time to smell the roses, enjoy the journey and make memories with those you love.*

Balance & Taking Care of Yourself

Work hard and play hard.

Genesis 2

2 And on the seventh day God ended his work which he had made; and he rested on the seventh day from all his work which he had made.

_____

_____

_____

_____

_____

Even God found time to rest! Do the best possible job you can while at work, but also do your best to reward and replenish yourself when you are away from work. Your body will thank you for it.

Balance & Taking Care of Yourself

Remember to be good to yourself.

Ecclesiastes 5

[18] Here is what I have seen: It is good and fitting for one to eat and drink, and to enjoy the good of all his labor in which he toils under the sun all the days of his life which God gives him; for it is his heritage.

What good does it do to spend your life taking care of others, while your body falls apart? Remember the little things that make you smile, and commit to reward yourself with those things frequently.

Balance & Taking Care of Yourself

You cannot birth the promise effectively if you are
"weak" in self!

Psalm 18
[32] It is God that girdeth me with strength, and maketh my way perfect.

_____

_____

_____

_____

_____

*Your welfare is top priority because if you are not strong and sound, you will not be able to birth the
dream God has stored inside of you. Restore your body and soul so that you can deliver that dream!*

Balance & Taking Care of Yourself

Learn to laugh – you will live longer.

Psalm 126

2 Then was our mouth filled with laughter, and our tongue with singing: then said they among the heathen, The LORD hath done great things for them.

_____

_____

_____

_____

_____

Laughter is not only good for you, it is also a tremendous testimony to anyone around you who does not know of the Father's love and His ability to sustain you through anything. Let your laughter speak for you today.

Balance & Taking Care of Yourself

If it doesn't fit, don't force it.

Exodus 18

[18] Both you and these people who are with you will surely wear yourselves out. For this thing is too much for you; you are not able to perform it by yourself. (NKJV)

_____

_____

_____

_____

_____

Why are you adding more items to your "To Do" list before crossing anything off? Make a decision today to limit your commitments to only those items you can handle without sacrificing your sanity!

Balance & Taking Care of Yourself

Life has to be managed to be effective.

1 Corinthians 14
[33] For He [Who is the source of their prophesying] is not a God of confusion and disorder but of peace and order. As [is the practice] in all the churches of the saints (God's people)…(AMP)

God's example to us was consistent peace and order.
Manage your life by using lists and calendars and the word "NO" as much as necessary.

Balance & Taking Care of Yourself

If you are empty, you have nothing to give
– you give what you have.

Jeremiah 12

5 [But the Lord rebukes Jeremiah's impatience, saying] If you have raced with men on foot and they have tired you out, then how can you compete with horses? (AMP)

_____

_____

_____

_____

_____

Your inability to manage life effectively can lead to chaos – not only in your natural surroundings, but in the Spirit realm, as well. Make sure you take the time to be ministered to, so that your ministry can thrive.

Balance & Taking Care of Yourself

People always return to a place of pleasure
(create pleasure in your home).

Proverbs 14
[1] EVERY WISE woman builds her house, but the foolish one tears
it down with her own hands

_____

_____

_____

_____

_____

Is your house a safe haven to rest in? It should be a welcoming environment that embraces
you and shelters you from the harshness of the world.

Balance & Taking Care of Yourself

It's the "little" things that mean the most
– it's where you draw the strength or lose it.

Ecclesiastes 9

[7] Go your way, eat your bread with joy, and drink your wine with a cheerful heart [if you are righteous, wise, and in the hands of God], for God has already accepted your works.

_____

_____

_____

_____

_____

It doesn't take much to reward yourself. But whatever it is – a favorite food, movie, place – treat yourself to that thing every now and then to help replenish your spirit and mind.

Balance & Taking Care of Yourself

There is a difference between getting a blessing and being a blessing. You can't be what you haven't got.

Ecclesiastes 3

[13] And also that every man should eat and drink, and enjoy the good of all his labour, it is the gift of God.

God's gift to you is the ability to enjoy the fruit of your labor – and to be able to bless others with that fruit. If you have been too busy to pick the fruit, who can you feed?

Balance & Taking Care of Yourself

You have to give yourself what you wish from others.

Matthew 6
[33] But seek ye first the kingdom of God, and his righteousness;
and all these things shall be added unto you.

First, take care of your personal needs for love and fulfillment through God. Then, He will equip you with those same gifts to share with others.

Self Esteem

God precisely and perfectly made you.

Matthew 10
[30] But the very hairs of your head are all numbered.

_____

_____

_____

_____

_____

You are exactly what God wanted you to be from head to toe. You are the "right" gender, race, personality, body shape, and height to accomplish the dream that He has for you. You are already equipped with all you will ever need.

Self Esteem

You are distinctively and necessarily different.

Psalm 139
[14] I will praise thee; for I am fearfully and wonderfully made…

_____

_____

_____

_____

_____

It's an awesome feeling to realize that God is aware of every aspect of us that makes us unique.
You are who you are for a very distinct and unique purpose.
Thank God today for making you a designer original.

Self Esteem

Greatest enemy you have is your "inner me."

2 Corinthians 10

[12] For we dare not make ourselves of the number, or compare ourselves with some that commend themselves: but they measuring themselves by themselves, and comparing themselves among themselves, are not wise.

_____

_____

_____

_____

_____

Don't be your own worst critic. Be your own best supporter. God has made you divinely perfect; so you have no right to make yourself feel any less than you really are.

Self Esteem

When we deal with others, we do so by reaching into our own well of self-esteem, and we treat them from that supply.

Proverbs 5

[15] Drink waters out of thine own cistern, and running waters out of thine own well.

How can you love anyone else if you do not love yourself? Seek God to gain true appreciation and love for yourself, then you can love others from that supply.

Self Esteem

Recognize that those who reject you have no ability to see inside you.

Mark 12

[10] Have you not even read this [passage of] Scripture: The very Stone which [after putting It to the test] the builders rejected has become the Head of the corner [Cornerstone];

Other people's inability to appreciate you should never slow you down.
Where would we be today if Jesus had been swayed by His persecutors?

Self Esteem

Your stutter won't stop your anointing (Moses).

Exodus 4

¹⁰ And Moses said to the Lord, O Lord, I am not eloquent or a man of words, neither before nor since You have spoken to Your servant; for I am slow of speech and have a heavy and awkward tongue.

_____

_____

_____

_____

_____

God has already equipped you with everything you need to fulfill the purpose He has for you. What you see as an impediment may be the very thing that God has chosen to use for His good.

Self Esteem

The you that you see is the you that you'll become.

Genesis 1

26 And God said, Let us make man in our image, after our likeness:

You have been made in the image of Christ. If you do not see yourself that way, adjust your perception. If you see yourself as anything less, that's all you will ever be.

Self Esteem

Until you accept that God created you perfectly as you are, you
will try to be someone else, and that would be an imitation.

Philippians 1

[6] Being confident of this very thing, that he which hath begun a good work in you will
perform it until the day of Jesus Christ:

Take some time today to thank God for making you just as you are.
No one else could be You as well as you can. And, you can never be anyone else.

Self Esteem

It is your differences that make you so valuable.

Ephesians 2

[10] For we are his workmanship, created in Christ Jesus unto good works, which God hath before ordained that we should walk in them.

_____

_____

_____

_____

_____

God has precisely made you to be the distinct person you are, born of two designated parents, and birthed on the exact day and time that He commanded. That alone makes you an invaluable gift to the world.

Self Esteem

You are the 67th book of the Bible - a living epistle.

2 Corinthians 3

2 Ye are our epistle written in our hearts, known and read of all men:

You are a walking testament to the goodness and grace of God.
He has performed a marvelous work in you that should be shared with the world.

Self Esteem

It is therapeutic to know that God likes me and
accepts me even if no one else does.

Eph 1

6 To the praise of the glory of his grace, wherein he hath made
us accepted in the beloved.

_____

_____

_____

_____

_____

Find comfort in God's love and acceptance. His is the only opinion that will matter in the end.

Self Esteem

If you don't value yourself – no one else will.

2 Corinthians 4

[7] But we have this treasure in earthen vessels, that the excellency of
the power may be of God, and not of us.

_____

_____

_____

_____

_____

*God has placed tremendous power inside of you – His power. The more you realize how
precious you are in His sight, the more others will see just how valuable you are.*

You are filled with endless potential and possibilities.

Philippians 4
[13] I can do all things through Christ which strengtheneth me.

There is no limit to what you can accomplish through Christ. The only thing holding you back is you!

Self Esteem

You are not a product of what you went through or what you did.

Luke 15

21 And the son said unto him, Father, I have sinned against heaven, and in thy sight, and am no more worthy to be called thy son.

You are only a product of what God has proclaimed over you. Stand tall and rejoice in the fact that God's love has purified you and erased all of your past sins. Start over today with a clean slate.

Faith

If you can see the invisible, you can do the impossible.

Hebrews 11
[1] Now faith is the substance of things hoped for,
the evidence of things not seen.

_____

_____

_____

_____

_____

It's been said that things you cannot see are more real than the things you can see because everything
originated as something you could not see. You were once only a thought or a dream –
but now you are a reality. See your future as limitless, and it will be.

Faith

The only job you have is to believe God can do His job!

Matthew 6

30 Wherefore, if God so clothe the grass of the field, which to day is, and tomorrow is cast into the oven, shall he not much more clothe you, O ye of little faith?

Give your cares to God today and allow Him to do just what He desires to – to protect and bless you.

Faith

Faith is a lifestyle that you are to live by.

Habakkuk 2

4   Behold, his soul which is lifted up is not upright in him:
but the just shall live by his faith.

_____

_____

_____

_____

_____

Faith is not just a feeling or thought – it is a lifestyle.
It includes a change of mindset from "maybe" to "definitely".

Faith

When faith graduates, it becomes trust.

Luke 16

[12] And if ye have not been faithful in that which is another man's,
who shall give you that which is your own?

_____

_____

_____

_____

_____

*As your faith is continuously tested, it will grow and mature into
trusting God for anything that you will ever need.*

Faith

Faith takes you from promise to performance.

Galatians 3

[14] That the blessing of Abraham might come on the Gentiles through Jesus Christ; that we might receive the promise of the Spirit through faith.

_____

_____

_____

_____

_____

Your faithfulness provokes God to act on your behalf.
Stand firm in unwavering faith, and watch God amaze you.

Faith

It's better to move in faith than to sit in doubt.

2 Corinthians 5

7 For we walk by faith, not by sight.

_____

_____

_____

_____

_____

Faithfully step out on the Word that God has placed in your heart. He will be sure to catch you.

Faith

It takes faith and patience to inherit the promise.

Matthew 25

21 His lord said unto him, Well done, thou good and faithful servant: thou hast been faithful over a few things, I will make thee ruler over many things: enter thou into the joy of thy lord.

_____

_____

_____

_____

_____

It's not enough to say you believe God is going to work things out. You must have unyielding faith as you patiently expect His promise.

Faith

Unbelief is a sin by which we greatly dishonor God.

Matthew 14

[31] And immediately Jesus stretched forth his hand, and caught him, and said unto him, O thou of little faith, wherefore didst thou doubt?

_____

_____

_____

_____

_____

Don't insult God by doubting Him. Resist doubt and embrace a spirit of expectation today!

Faith

Faith is the anointing connector

Matthew 15

28   Then Jesus answered and said unto her, O woman, great is thy faith: be it unto thee even as thou wilt. And her daughter was made whole from that very hour.

_____

_____

_____

_____

_____

Miraculous works have been borne out of great faith.
When you mix your faith with the awesome anointing of God, anything is possible.

Faith

Faith is what moves God.

Matthew 8
[10] When Jesus heard it, he marvelled, and said to them that followed, Verily I say unto you, I have not found so great faith, no, not in Israel.

Can you imagine making Jesus marvel? That is what great faith does.
It impresses God so much, He is moved to act on your behalf!

Faith

You can only operate in faith according to your knowledge of His will or desire for your life.

Romans 4

20 He staggered not at the promise of God through unbelief; but was strong in faith, giving glory to God;

_____

_____

_____

_____

_____

Perfect faith cannot exist where the will of God is unknown. How can you know God's will for your life if you do not seek Him? Spend time alone with God today so you can know if what you are seeking is in line with what He has for you.

Faith

My faith has been developed by the Word that has been deposited.

Romans 10

[8] But what saith it? The word is nigh thee, even in thy mouth, and in thy heart: that is, the word of faith, which we preach;

[17] So then faith cometh by hearing, and hearing by the word of God.

_____

_____

_____

_____

_____

How can you seek God in faith if you do not know what He can do for you? Study God's Word to understand the vastness of His ability to provide for your every need.

Faith

The distinction of a real leader is the dimension
of faith he or she has.

Matthew 17

[20] And Jesus said unto them, Because of your unbelief: for verily I say unto you, If
ye have faith as a grain of mustard seed, ye shall say unto this mountain, Remove
hence to yonder place; and it shall remove; and nothing shall be impossible unto
you.

_____

_____

_____

_____

_____

*A leader without faith is a blind follower. If you do not believe,
how can you lead others to believe in you?*

Faith

If you don't have anything to hope for,
you have no use for faith.

1 Samuel 17
[29] …Is there not a cause?

_____

_____

_____

_____

_____

Your faith is wasted if you have no cause to believe in. Put your trust in God and
your faith in the works that He will surely commit in your life.

Healing & Coping

God will birth a miracle out of your mess.

Genesis 50

20   But as for you, ye thought evil against me; but God meant it unto good, to bring to pass, as it is this day, to save much people alive.

In the midst of your situation, God will step in and turn things around to work in your favor.
Lean on Him today in the assurance that He can heal and mend any place of infirmity in your life.

Healing & Coping

Tough times are an opportunity to grow.

Psalm 34

¹⁸ The LORD is close to the brokenhearted and saves those who are crushed in spirit.

_____

_____

_____

_____

_____

This situation may be just the delay you need to reevaluate the direction you are in. Seek God for comfort and direction as you take the time to reflect on the lessons you have learned.

Healing & Coping

God prepared you for this time before you were released.

Esther 4

[14] …And who knows but that you have come to the kingdom for such a time as this and for this very occasion?

If God knew you and planted a seed of destiny in you before the beginning of time, doesn't it stand to reason that He has also prepared you for this moment? Just as He prepared you to get to this place, He has given you all that you need to get through this place.

Healing & Coping

Your circumstances are hindrances to seeing God's abilities.

John 20

[10] Then the disciples went away again unto their own home.

[11] But Mary stood without at the sepulchre weeping: and as she wept, she stooped down, and looked into the sepulchre, [12] And seeth two angels in white sitting, the one at the head, and the other at the feet, where the body of Jesus had lain. [13] And they say unto her, Woman, why weepest thou? She saith unto them, Because they have taken away my LORD, and I know not where they have laid him. [14] And when she had thus said, she turned herself back, and saw Jesus standing, and knew not that it was Jesus.

_____

_____

_____

_____

_____

Mary was so distraught about Jesus' death that she did not recognize Him when she saw Him. She was so caught up in the problem, that she couldn't see the Problem Solver. Don't let anything distract you from seeing God's awesome ability to heal and restore you.

Healing & Coping

Allow God's love to pierce through your pain.

Romans 5

⁸ But God commendeth his love toward us, in that,
while we were yet sinners, Christ died for us.

_____

_____

_____

_____

_____

Christ's love is deeper than anything you have ever known.
Give Him the chance to heal your pain through His perfect love.

Healing & Coping

The only difference between black coal and precious diamond is the amount of pressure it endured.

Hebrews 12

³ Just think of Him Who endured from sinners such grievous opposition and bitter hostility against Himself [reckon up and consider it all in comparison with your trials], so that you may not grow weary or exhausted, losing heart and relaxing and fainting in your minds. (AMP)

Jesus endured more than you ever will – all to give you eternal salvation. Don't reject His gift to you by giving up hope when things get tough. Trust Him to see you through your trial, as He always does.

Healing & Coping

If you ever lost anything, it's only because of
God that you didn't lose everything.

Psalm 136
16   To him which led his people through the wilderness:
for his mercy endureth for ever.

_____

_____

_____

_____

_____

God's unending mercy is what has sustained you through your toughest times.
Be thankful for making it this far, and for what you know He is about to do for you.

Healing & Coping

Don't bypass the process for the progress.

2 Corinthians 3
[18] But we all, with open face beholding as in a glass the glory of the Lord, are changed into the same image from glory to glory, even as by the Spirit of the Lord.

_____

_____

_____

_____

_____

The journey towards progress is very important. There is purpose in every process, so don't despise what you have to go through. Take the time to ask God to help you understand what you are supposed to learn in your situation, instead of praying to be released from it.

Treasure of the Day

Paula White

Healing & Coping

Who can wipe a tear that will not fall?

Revelation 7

[17] For the Lamb at the center of the throne will be their shepherd;
he will lead them to springs of living water.
And God will wipe away every tear from their eyes." (NIV)

In order to truly heal, you must first face the pain built up inside of you.
You may not have to literally cry, but you will have to release all the bottled up pain that is
keeping you from moving forward. God will comfort you and wipe your tears away.

Healing & Coping

Healing has occurred when you remember the tragic events of
yesterday but feel no pain.

Matthew 9
[22] But Jesus turned him about, and when he saw her, he said, Daughter,
be of good comfort; thy faith hath made thee whole.
And the woman was made whole from that hour.

_____

_____

_____

_____

_____

When God heals you, you are able to remember your pain,
but only for the sake of telling your testimony.

Healing & Coping

God's time to appear for His people is when their strength is gone.

1 Samuel 30

[6] David was greatly distressed because the men were talking of stoning him; each one was bitter in spirit because of his sons and daughters. But David found strength in the LORD his God.

_____

_____

_____

_____

_____

When you feel at your weakest point, trust in God to support you and cradle you in His perfect strength.

Healing & Coping

God's peace comforts you from the harsh realities of life.

Philippians 4

7 And the peace of God, which passeth all understanding,
shall keep your hearts and minds through Christ Jesus.

_____

_____

_____

_____

_____

*The peace of God is calmness in the middle of the storm. Rest in the comfort of knowing
that He is already at work mending your broken heart.*

Healing & Coping

Half the solution to any problem lies in defining how you got there.

2 Corinthians 12

[7] And to keep me from being puffed up and too much elated by the exceeding greatness (preeminence) of these revelations, there was given me a thorn (a splinter) in the flesh, a messenger of Satan, to rack and buffet and harass me, to keep me from being excessively exalted. (AMP)

_____

_____

_____

_____

_____

God engineered this adversity to keep Paul from exalting himself. Could it be that the journey you are on is meant to teach you something about yourself that you would never have realized otherwise?

Healing & Coping

A wound is an event. Healing is a process.

Psalm 23

[3] He restoreth my soul: he leadeth me in the paths of
righteousness for his name's sake.

_____

_____

_____

_____

_____

*Emotional healing does not happen overnight, but it does happen in time if you
are patient and allow God to work on your behalf. Cast your cares on Him and
He will restore you to better than you were before.*

Praise & Worship

You can't praise God and worry about a promotion; for when you begin to praise God, you have already been promoted.

Psalm 150
[6] Let everything that hath breath praise the Lord. Praise ye the Lord.

Continual praise is the key to receiving blessings beyond your imagination.
If you spend your thoughts and words on Praise, there will be no room for doubt.

Praise & Worship

**Complaining causes you to remain –
Praising causes you to be raised.**

Psalm 34

1 I will bless the LORD at all times: his praise shall continually be in my mouth.

---

*Negative words are cords that bind you where you are.
Praise lifts you out of your situation and into hope and peace and blessings.*

Praise & Worship

Polite applause is illegal praise.

Psalm 22
[22] I will declare thy name unto my brethren:
in the midst of the congregation will I praise thee.

To discreetly thank God for all that He has done is an insult to Him in light of all that He has done for you. Praise Him outwardly, and He will bless you outwardly.

Praise & Worship

One of the few things God ever sought was a worshipper.

John 4

23 But the hour cometh, and now is, when the true worshippers shall worship the Father in spirit and in truth: for the Father seeketh such to worship him.

_____

_____

_____

_____

_____

What a privilege it is to offer yourself up as the very thing that God sought after!
Worship Him now with your whole heart to show just how much He means to you.

Praise & Worship

Your victory is in your praise.

2 Chronicles 20

21 And when he had consulted with the people, he appointed singers unto the LORD, and that should praise the beauty of holiness, as they went out before the army, and to say, Praise the LORD; for his mercy endureth for ever.

22 And when they began to sing and to praise, the LORD set ambushments against the children of Ammon, Moab, and mount Seir, which were come against Judah; and they were smitten.

When you praise God in the midst of your situation, you are telling Him that you trust that He has already given you the victory over that situation. Your praise is rooted in faith, and faith moves God.

Praise & Worship

Spectators don't get trophies.

1 Chronicles 16
[25] For great is the LORD, and greatly to be praised:
he also is to be feared above all gods.

_____

_____

_____

_____

_____

Standing by and watching others praise and worship God does not draw you closer to Him. True intimacy with God is established when you are lifting your voice and bending your knees to Him.

Praise & Worship

Your enemies have done more for you than all of your friends…they have taught you to praise.

2 Samuel 22

4 I will call on the LORD, who is worthy to be praised: so shall I be saved from mine enemies.

50 Therefore I will give thanks unto thee, O LORD, among the heathen, and I will sing praises unto thy name.

_____

_____

_____

_____

_____

If you never had adversity, you would not appreciate deliverance. If you had never been delivered, you would not know how to praise God for making a way!

Praise & Worship

He blesses those who praise Him.

Psalm 106
1 Praise the LORD! Oh, give thanks to the LORD, for He is good!
For His mercy endures forever.

_____

_____

_____

_____

_____

Your praise is the key to your blessings in Christ. Lift up your voice and honor the King of Kings, and He will reward you for your praise.

Praise & Worship

When you worship God, you denote
His worthiness and worthship.

1 Chronicles 16

²⁹ Give unto the LORD the glory due unto his name: bring an offering, and come
before him: worship the LORD in the beauty of holiness.

_____

_____

_____

_____

_____

Worship is your opportunity to tell God how much He means to you and who he is to you.
Never let a day go by without spending time telling God who He is to you.

Praise & Worship

True worship begins when true sacrifice occurs.

2 Kings 17

[36] But the LORD, who brought you up out of the land of Egypt with
great power and a stretched out arm, him shall ye fear,
and him shall ye worship, and to him shall ye do sacrifice.

_____

_____

_____

_____

_____

When you sacrifice anything to spend time with God, it brings you closer to Him.
It says to Him that he means more to you than that thing you went without.
What can you sacrifice today to come one step closer to Him?

Praise & Worship

Praise will make a weary man perform.

Psalm 21

[13] Be thou exalted, LORD, in thine own strength: so will we sing and praise thy power.

_____

_____

_____

_____

_____

In the natural, even the most exhausted person can be persuaded to help you if you give them praises.

Praise & Worship

God is not just a God who gives.
He also receives. He receives our worship.

2 Chronicles 5

[13] It came even to pass, as the trumpeters and singers were as one, to make one sound
to be heard in praising and thanking the LORD; and when they lifted up their voice
with the trumpets and cymbals and instruments of musick, and praised the LORD,
saying, For he is good; for his mercy endureth for ever: that then the house was filled
with a cloud, even the house of the LORD;

_____

_____

_____

_____

_____

What an honor to be able to give to God who gives to us without ceasing!
The time to give the gift of worship to God is today.

Praise & Worship

You cannot dwell in the darkness of yesterday if you are
going to see the light of tomorrow.

Psalm 9
[1]   I will praise thee, O LORD, with my whole heart;
I will shew forth all thy marvellous works.

_____

_____

_____

_____

_____

*PRAISE! PRAISE! PRAISE! That is the key to moving past the pain of yesterday and into the
promise of tomorrow. Thank Him now for the awesome healing He is about to perform in your life!*

Praise & Worship

Praise is thanking God for what He has done.
Worship is expressing who God is.

Psalm 138

2 I will worship toward thy holy temple, and praise thy name for thy lovingkindness
and for thy truth: for thou hast magnified thy word above all thy name.

Praise and worship are essential components of a healthy relationship with God.
They are necessary to build intimacy and hear from Him for direction.
Don't deny God the very things that He made you to do!

Obedience & Discipline

Disobedience to God's Word brings destruction.

Deuteronomy 11

28 And a curse, if ye will not obey the commandments of the LORD your God,
but turn aside out of the way which I command you this day,
to go after other gods, which ye have not known.

As any good parent does, God brings correction to us when we disobey Him.
The only sure way to avoid correction is through obedience.
Choose today to be an obedient child of God so that you can experience the fullness of His love.

Obedience & Discipline

Every human was born with two agendas:
(1) God's, (2) Enemy's.

Romans 7

[19] For I fail to practice the good deeds I desire to do, but the evil deeds that I do not desire to do are what I am [ever] doing.

_____

_____

_____

_____

_____

Each of us struggles with fleshly temptations that try to lure us away from what we know to be right.
Make the choice daily to resist your flesh and follow God's direction.
Only He can lead you to eternal life.

Obedience & Discipline

What you do daily becomes a habit.

Jeremiah 13

23 Can the Ethiopian change his skin, or the leopard his spots?
then may ye also do good, that are accustomed to do evil.

_____

_____

_____

_____

_____

The bible says it is very difficult for one who is accustomed to doing evil to do good. Make consistent daily efforts to grow in obedience to God's Word so that doing good becomes your lifestyle, and doing evil becomes a thing of the past.

Obedience & Discipline

Your future is found in your daily routine.

Galatians 5

[16] But I say, walk and live [habitually] in the [Holy] Spirit [responsive to and controlled and guided by the Spirit]; then you will certainly not gratify the cravings and desires of the flesh (of human nature without God).

_____

_____

_____

_____

_____

What do you do consistently everyday? Even the smallest action, if done often enough, can drastically effect your life. Be mindful of negative habits that could have long-term effects on your health, wealth, or salvation. Re-evaluate your habits today. Your life could depend on it.

Obedience & Discipline

Successful people do daily what others do occasionally.

Deuteronomy 8

[1] "Be careful to obey all the commands I am giving you today. Then you will live and multiply, and you will enter and occupy the land the LORD swore to give your ancestors.

Just as consistent negative habits can lead to destruction, positive habits such as prayer, praise and worship can lead you to a deeper relationship with Christ and abundant living that He has for you. Make Jesus your habit – you will never regret it.

Obedience & Discipline

To be disciplined means to do the right thing when you feel like doing the wrong thing.

1 John 3

[9] Whosoever is born of God doth not commit sin; for his seed remaineth in him: and he cannot sin, because he is born of God.

_____

_____

_____

_____

_____

Your flesh will often not agree with doing the "right" thing because it's often easier to do the "wrong" thing. True discipline requires you to follow the Holy Spirit – not your flesh.

Obedience & Discipline

Promotion comes as a result of faithfulness.

1 Peter 5

[6] Therefore humble yourselves under the mighty hand of God,
that He may exalt you in due time.　(NKJV)

_____

_____

_____

_____

_____

*When you are faithful, you are consistent and unwavering in your dedication. God rewards that
dedication because it is proof to Him that He can trust you with His blessings.*

Obedience & Discipline

You don't have to die to face the consequences of
your decisions – you live with them daily.

Psalm 119
30　I have chosen the way of truth: thy judgments have I laid before me.

_____

_____

_____

_____

_____

*Poor choices always lead to negative consequences. The decisions you make today can
have effects that last for years. Make the decision to follow God and His precepts,
and you will feast on the fruit of that decision forever.*

233

Obedience & Discipline

The pain of discipline weighs much less than the heavy load of regret.

2 Corinthians 7

[10] Godly sorrow brings repentance that leads to salvation and leaves no regret, but worldly sorrow brings death.

_____

_____

_____

_____

_____

In the end, obedience is an easier choice to make because it carries no regrets or negative consequences. Treat yourself to the rewards of the Holy Spirit by diligently following Him and allowing Him to take you to new levels in your walk with Him.

Obedience & Discipline

Don't pursue what the Holy Ghost has already rejected in your life.

1 Peter 2

[8] And the Scriptures also say, "He is the stone that makes people stumble, the rock that will make them fall." They stumble because they do not listen to God's word or obey it, and so they meet the fate that has been planned for them. (NLT)

When God closes a door, let it remain closed. Your forcing it open can only lead to frustration and disappointment. Trust that He will never close a door without opening another one.

Obedience & Discipline

If the enemy can't get you to quit, he will get you distracted.

1 Corinthians 7

35 And this I speak for your own profit; not that I may cast a snare upon you, but for that which is comely, and that ye may attend upon the Lord without distraction.

_____

_____

_____

_____

_____

Focus is the key to obedience. Remain focused on God, and all distractions will fade away.

Obedience & Discipline

Use the areas that are working for you to correct
the areas that are not working.

Genesis 35

[11] And God said unto him, I am God Almighty: be fruitful and multiply; a nation and a
company of nations shall be of thee, and kings shall come out of thy loins;

_____

_____

_____

_____

_____

*When God commands you to be fruitful, He makes you seedful. Identify the seeds of
greatness in your life and build on them.*

Obedience & Discipline

His last command is our first priority
(The Great Commission – not suggestion).

Matthew 28

[19] Go ye therefore, and teach all nations, baptizing them in the name of the Father, and of the Son, and of the Holy Ghost:

[20] Teaching them to observe all things whatsoever I have commanded you: and, lo, I am with you always, even unto the end of the world. Amen.

We are all called to spread the Word of God to anyone who is willing to listen.
Share the good news of the gospel and watch the Holy Spirit transform
lives and deliver them from darkness and into marvelous light.

Obedience & Discipline

Challenge yourself out of your comfort zone
and into your commitment zone.

1 Kings 22

[43] And he walked in all the ways of Asa his father; he turned not aside from it, doing that which was right in the eyes of the LORD: nevertheless the high places were not taken away; for the people offered and burnt incense yet in the high places.

_____

_____

_____

_____

_____

True discipline requires you to remove yourself from that which is most comfortable,
and transition into what is the will of God. It may not be comfortable to your flesh,
but consider it "growing pains" for your soul as you mature spiritually.

Valley of Decision

The quality of your decisions will determine the quality of your life.

Joshua 24

[15] And if it seem evil unto you to serve the LORD, choose you this day whom ye will serve; whether the gods which your fathers served that were on the other side of the flood, or the gods of the Amorites, in whose land ye dwell: but as for me and my house, we will serve the LORD.

_____

_____

_____

_____

_____

The most important decision you will ever make is the decision to serve Christ with all of your heart. Once you make that decision, every aspect of your life is touched. You receive the clarity of heart and mind to see through any situation or decision that comes your way.

Valley of Decision

Live tomorrow what you decide today.

Genesis 8
22 While the earth remaineth, seedtime and harvest, and cold and heat, and summer and winter, and day and night shall not cease.

The seeds you sow today determines the harvest you will reap tomorrow.
Sow seeds of kindness, love, generosity and goodness today.

Valley of Decision

Everything you decide is a preview of your future.

Isaiah 56

³ Neither let the son of the stranger, that hath joined himself to the LORD, speak, saying, The LORD hath utterly separated me from his people: neither let the eunuch say, Behold, I am a dry tree.

⁴ For thus saith the LORD unto the eunuchs that keep my sabbaths, and choose the things that please me, and take hold of my covenant;

⁵ Even unto them will I give in mine house and within my walls a place and a name better than of sons and of daughters: I will give them an everlasting name, that shall not be cut off.

_____

_____

_____

_____

_____

If you act carelessly, sooner or later, your actions will catch up with you. That is true about all areas of your life - your eating and spending habits, your attitude, your sexual morality, and your walk with God. Make sure that the decisions you make paint a pretty picture of your future.

Valley of Decision

Even a decision not to choose is a decision.

2 Chronicles 13

[7] Some worthless scoundrels gathered around him and opposed Rehoboam son of Solomon when he was young and indecisive and not strong enough to resist them.

_____

_____

_____

_____

_____

When you do not make decisions for yourself, you give others the right to decide your fate for you.
Make a habit of pursuing God for any answers you are seeking today,
and He will help you to be definitive in all that you do.

Valley of Decision

A lack of decisiveness has caused more failures than a lack of intelligence.

Genesis 19

[15] At dawn the next morning the angels became insistent. "Hurry," they said to Lot. "Take your wife and your two daughters who are here. Get out of here right now, or you will be caught in the destruction of the city."

[16] When Lot still hesitated, the angels seized his hand and the hands of his wife and two daughters and rushed them to safety outside the city, for the LORD was merciful.

_____

_____

_____

_____

The time you spend trying to make a decision may be all the time you have to act on it. When you are in line with God's will for your life, you are able to quickly discern which decisions compliment your goal, and which ones cripple your goal so that you can pursue only those things that will strengthen your walk with Him.

Valley of Decision

If you cannot enjoy a memory, then don't make a decision.

1 Timothy 6

[10] For the love of money is a root of all kinds of evil. Some people, eager for money, have wandered from the faith and pierced themselves with many griefs. NIV

_____

_____

_____

_____

_____

Who wants to pierce themselves with many griefs? When you deliberately make a decision to do something that will bring you harsh circumstances, you set yourself up for pain and grief in the future.

Valley of Decision

We are the sum total of the choices we make every day.

Proverbs 3
[31] Envy thou not the oppressor, and choose none of his ways.

Be keenly aware of the choices you make every day.
They will all add up to equate to the life that you live.

Valley of Decision

The greatest demand on us daily is decisions.

Joel 3

[14] Multitudes, multitudes in the valley of decision: for the day of the LORD is near in the valley of decision.

_____

_____

_____

_____

_____

Everything you do every day you live will involve decision-making.
Your ability to handle the process by allowing God to direct you through the valley
of decision will make all the difference in where you end up when you exit.

Valley of Decision

The power to choose is the responsibility of choice.

Proverbs 1
[29] Since they hated knowledge
and did not choose to fear the LORD,
[30] since they would not accept my advice
and spurned my rebuke,
[31] they will eat the fruit of their ways
and be filled with the fruit of their schemes.

_____

_____

_____

_____

_____

If we didn't have power to choose, we would not be responsible to choose. With the responsibility of choice comes the accountability to make sound choices that effect your life positively.

Valley of Decision

Don't ever make a permanent decision in a temporary situation.

Isaiah 65

¹² Therefore will I number you to the sword, and ye shall all bow down to the slaughter: because when I called, ye did not answer; when I spake, ye did not hear; but did evil before mine eyes, and did choose that wherein I delighted not.

_____

_____

_____

_____

_____

No matter how you feel in the flesh, take a moment to seek God before making a rash decision. You cannot see all of your options clearly until you ask God for revelation over the situation.

Valley of Decision

God will always give you another chance:
the choice is yours to take it.

Deuteronomy 30
[19] I call heaven and earth to record this day against you,
that I have set before you life and death, blessing and cursing:
therefore choose life, that both thou and thy seed may live:

_____

_____

_____

_____

_____

God sees beyond what you have done, and looks at what you can do through His love. When you make
poor choices, listen for the Holy Spirit to guide you back to the path that God has for you.

Valley of Decision

Choice, not chance, determines destiny.

Job 34

[4] Let us choose to us judgment: let us know among ourselves what is good.

You have the awesome power to accomplish anything you want to through the choices you make.
Choose today to achieve the divine destiny that God has in store for you.

Valley of Decision

You are a product of your decisions.

Isaiah 7
[15] Butter and honey shall he eat, that he may know to refuse the evil,
and choose the good.

_____

_____

_____

_____

_____

Laziness and procrastination are choices.
Choose today to be efficient and productive and motivated!

Valley of Decision

When your heart decides a destination,
your mind will design a map to reach it.

Matthew 4

[21] Going on from there, he saw two other brothers, James son of Zebedee and his brother John. They were in a boat with their father Zebedee, preparing their nets. Jesus called them,

[22] and immediately they left the boat and their father and followed him. (NIV)

_____

_____

_____

_____

_____

*Choose today to drop everything that would hinder you
and follow Christ will all of your heart and mind.*

Favor

Favor is undeserved access.

Genesis 6
[8] But Noah found favor in the eyes of the LORD.

_____

_____

_____

_____

_____

*The favor of God will give you access to places you could not
have earned through years of education or influence.*

Favor

Favor will take you from your present season to your future destination.

Esther 2

[17] Now the king was attracted to Esther more than to any of the other women, and she won his favor and approval more than any of the other virgins. So he set a royal crown on her head and made her queen instead of Vashti.

_____

_____

_____

_____

_____

Through the favor of God, your situation can be transformed in the blink of an eye.

Favor

Favor is worth 1,000 days of labor in your life.

Proverbs 19

[12] The king's wrath is as the roaring of a lion; but his favour is as dew upon the grass.

How sweet it is to experience the unmatched, unearned favor of God!

Favor

Favor isn't fair.

Genesis 4

3 In the course of time Cain brought some of the fruits of the soil as an offering to the LORD.

4 But Abel brought fat portions from some of the firstborn of his flock. The LORD looked with favor on Abel and his offering,

5 but on Cain and his offering he did not look with favor. So Cain was very angry, and his face was downcast. (NIV)

_____

_____

_____

_____

_____

God grants His favor in ways that man cannot understand. Be thankful when God smiles on you with favor because He could have chosen anyone else but you.

Favor

Favor will do for you what your money, your mate and your ministry can't do.

Proverbs 16

[15] When the king smiles, there is life; his favor refreshes like a gentle rain. (NIV)

———————————————————

———————————————————

———————————————————

———————————————————

———————————————————

Favor opens doors and changes hearts like you never could on your own. When favor is at work, you see supernatural, seemingly impossible things become commonplace.

Favor

Favor will move you from the pit to the palace.

Genesis 39

[21] the LORD was with him; he showed him kindness and granted him favor in the eyes of the prison warden.

[22] So the warden put Joseph in charge of all those held in the prison, and he was made responsible for all that was done there.

[23] The warden paid no attention to anything under Joseph's care, because the LORD was with Joseph and gave him success in whatever he did.

_____

_____

_____

_____

_____

Favor can turn any situation completely around so drastically that you will know it was God and not you.

Favor

Favor will cause your enemies to bless you.

Psalm 23
[5] Thou preparest a table before me in the presence of mine enemies: thou anointest my head with oil; my cup runneth over.

_____

_____

_____

_____

_____

God's favor will change the heart of your greatest adversaries so that they will feel driven to bless you and help you.

Favor

Favor will make your name great.

Genesis 17

15 Then God said to Abraham, "As for Sarai your wife, you shall not call her name Sarai, but Sarah shall be her name.

16 "And I will bless her and also give you a son by her; then I will bless her, and she shall be a mother of nations; kings of peoples shall be from her."

_____

_____

_____

_____

_____

Common people become people of great influence through God's favor.

Favor

Favor will bring wealth to you.

Leviticus 26

[9] "I will look on you with favor and make you fruitful and increase your
numbers, and I will keep my covenant with you."

---

*When God's favor is present, things that you worked all your life for
will walk into your life without you trying.*

Favor

Favor has to do with divine timing.

Psalm 102
13 You will arise and have compassion on Zion,
   for it is time to show favor to her;
   the appointed time has come.

_____

_____

_____

_____

_____

Favor has everything to do with God deciding to bless you tremendously when He chooses to, not when you think He will. You will see that His favor is right on time.

Favor

Favor brings promotion.

Psalm 75

6 For promotion cometh neither from the east, nor from the west, nor from the south.

7 But God is the judge: he putteth down one, and setteth up another.

_____

_____

_____

_____

_____

Promotion comes from God, and is the result of His divine favor and grace.
Don't wait on man to do for you what only God can.

Favor

Favor is the kiss of God on your life.

Psalm 5
[12] For surely, O LORD , you bless the righteous;
you surround them with your favor as with a shield.

The kiss of God will surround you and protect you, heal you and bless you all at once.

Favor

Favor is a result of the fear of the Lord.

Isaiah 33
[6] …the fear of the LORD is his treasure.

_____

_____

_____

_____

_____

You cannot have favor if you do not have reverence for the only One who can provide it.

Favor

Favor is when God blesses you out of order.

1 Samuel 16

¹⁰ Again, Jesse made seven of his sons to pass before Samuel. And Samuel said unto Jesse, The LORD hath not chosen these.

¹¹ And Samuel said unto Jesse, Are here all thy children? And he said, There remaineth yet the youngest, and, behold, he keepeth the sheep. And Samuel said unto Jesse, Send and fetch him: for we will not sit down till he come hither.

¹² And he sent, and brought him in. Now he was ruddy, and withal of a beautiful countenance, and goodly to look to. And the LORD said, Arise, anoint him: for this is he.

_____

_____

_____

_____

_____

Birthright and seniority mean nothing in the eyes of God when He chooses to bestow His awesome blessings upon you.

Walk with God

Joy is a product from God's presence.

Psalm 45
[7] You love righteousness and hate wickedness;
therefore God, your God, has set you above your companions
by anointing you with the oil of joy.

Indescribable joy and peace are the result of walking with
God daily through a lifestyle of righteousness.

Walk with God

You must daily derive your life from Him – Jesus – your fountain of living water.

2 Corinthians 4

[16] For which cause we faint not; but though our outward man perish, yet the inward man is renewed day by day.

_____

_____

_____

_____

_____

God will continue to restore and replenish you as you lean on Him daily as your living water and source of strength.

Treasure of the Day   *Paula White*

Walk with God

The real power of God is released when you experience it in a personal way.

Philippians 2

[13] For it is God which worketh in you both to will and to do of his good pleasure.

_____

_____

_____

_____

_____

As you build a relationship with God, His power will be released in your life and you will begin to see Him working through you.

Walk with God

Real depth of a relationship is established over time.

2 Samuel 13
[1] In the course of time, Amnon son of David fell in love with Tamar,
the beautiful sister of Absalom son of David.

_____

_____

_____

_____

_____

Just as human relationships develop over time, so must your relationship with God. It requires consistent, daily attention and devotion.

Walk with God

When you walk on water, you feel funny because it doesn't give your flesh support.

Matthew 14

[29] And he said, Come. And when Peter was come down out of the ship, he walked on the water, to go to Jesus. 30 But when he saw the wind boisterous, he was afraid; and beginning to sink, he cried, saying, Lord, save me.

Truly walking with God means that you completely yield to His will for you, and you begin to be led by the Holy Spirit.

Walk with God

You cannot break principles while pleading promises.

Hosea 12

6 Therefore turn thou to thy God: keep mercy and judgment,
and wait on thy God continually.

_____

_____

_____

_____

_____

As a Christian, we are held to live by the principles of God.
Your failure to uphold His principles dissolves your ability to reap of His promises.

Walk with God

When a person lives in the presence of the Lord, he has fixed
principles which rule his heart and guide his life.

1 Peter 2

[21] For even hereunto were ye called: because Christ also suffered for us,
leaving us an example, that ye should follow his steps.

_____

_____

_____

_____

_____

*If you are walking with God, you should have His principles etched on your
heart as guides for your daily life.*

Walk with God

God wants to deal with the "Real You."

2 Corinthians 5

[11] Knowing therefore the terror of the Lord, we persuade men;
but we are made manifest unto God;
and I trust also are made manifest in your consciences.

_____

_____

_____

_____

_____

When nobody else in the world understands you, God does.
Put down your facades and come to Him just as you are – just as He made you.

Walk with God

You must hear His voice until it becomes louder than any
other voice in your life.

Luke 8

15 "But the ones that fell on the good ground are those who, having heard the word
with a noble and good heart, keep it and bear fruit with patience.

_____

_____

_____

_____

_____

*Resist the voice of temptation or negativity and hearken unto His voice
as it leads you on your Christian walk.*

Walk with God

Stop living by what you feel and live by what God says.

Hebrews 10
[38] Now the just shall live by faith: but if any man draw back,
my soul shall have no pleasure in him.

_____

_____

_____

_____

_____

Walking in the flesh is not walking in agreement with what God has for you.
You can only hear Him speak if when you move into the spirit realm.

Walk with God

Walking in the Spirit means to be in synchronization with God.

Galatians 5

16 This I say then, Walk in the Spirit, and ye shall not fulfill the lust of the flesh.

To follow Christ means to be in sync with Him, not leading Him or leaving Him.
Allow God to lead you on the path of righteousness.

You can never exhaust revelation of a Word from God.

Proverbs 30

5   Every word of God is pure: he is a shield unto them that put their trust in him.

_____

_____

_____

_____

_____

God's Word withstands time and remains firm, regardless of your situation.
If you received a revelation from God, it will come to past because His word will never return void.

Walk with God

If you always please man, you will displease God.

Matthew 6

24 No man can serve two masters: for either he will hate the one, and love the other;
or else he will hold to the one, and despise the other.
Ye cannot serve God and mammon.

_____

_____

_____

_____

_____

God's will supercedes anything you think or feel. Yield to the will of
God and resist your flesh in order to perfect your walk with Him.

Walk with God

Pride pushes you out of the presence of God.

Romans 12

³ For I say, through the grace given unto me, to every man that is among you, not to think of himself more highly than he ought to think; but to think soberly, according as God hath dealt to every man the measure of faith.

_____

_____

_____

_____

_____

Do not allow pride to hinder you from hearing from God. Repent of prideful thoughts and ways today so that you can move closer to God.

Character

It doesn't matter what I go through in life –
but how I go through it.

Romans 5

3 And not only that, but we also glory in tribulations, knowing that tribulation produces perseverance; 4 and perseverance, character; and character, hope.

_____

_____

_____

_____

_____

*Pay close attention to how you react under pressure and in times of adversity.
That will reveal your level of character and also highlight areas of growth for you.*

Character

The building is only as tall as the foundation
is strong enough to build on.

Psalms 105

[19] Until the time that his word came to pass, The word of the LORD tested him.

---

*God tests to us help us build strength because He sees what our future holds and He knows what skills
we will need most to be successful in the future. If your integrity is constantly being tried, perhaps God is
preparing you for a place of extreme influence where you will need to operate in great integrity one day.*

Character

Meekness is controlled strength – not a weakness.

2 Corinthians 10

[1] Now I, Paul, myself am pleading with you by the meekness and gentleness of Christ--who in presence am lowly among you, but being absent am bold toward you.

_____

_____

_____

_____

_____

Meekness is a mildness of disposition and a gentleness of spirit that comes from knowing God and trusting in Him.

Character

You can have excellence without arrogance.

Isaiah 5

15   And the mean man is bowed down, and the great man is humbled,
and the eyes of the lofty are humbled:

_____

_____

_____

_____

_____

*Be confident in what God has blessed you with, while also maintaining a humble spirit.
When you lift yourself up in arrogance, you will eventually be brought back down to earth.*

Character

You cannot go beyond the limitations of your own character.

Deuteronomy 32

[20] And He said, My face will be veiled from them,
I will see what their end will be:
for they are an uncontrolled generation, children in whom is no faith.

God turns His face away from those who deliberately live without integrity.
He will not allow you to go any further than your character will sustain you.

Character

Right is right if no one is doing it,
and wrong is wrong if everyone is doing it.

Job 31

6   Let me be weighed in an even balance, that God may know mine integrity.

_____

_____

_____

_____

_____

In the midst of frivolity and sin, God will always see and reward those who maintain their integrity.

Character

Crisis does not make a person –
it simply exposes them to what they already are.

Deuteronomy 8

²   And thou shalt remember all the way which the LORD thy God led thee these forty years in the wilderness, to humble thee, and to prove thee, to know what was in thine heart, whether thou wouldest keep his commandments, or no.

_____

_____

_____

_____

_____

God will take you through a season of trial (wilderness) to expose your true character.

Character

Character is what you are; reputation is what
you try to make people believe you are.

Proverbs 20

7 The just man walketh in his integrity: his children are blessed after him.

_____

_____

_____

_____

_____

The godly walk in integrity and their integrity speaks for itself to produce a good reputation.

Character

A sign of maturity is when you make the right
choices during difficult times.

Hebrews 5

[14] But strong meat belongeth to them that are of full age,
even those who by reason of use have their senses exercised to
discern both good and evil.

_____

_____

_____

_____

_____

The Rhema Word of God causes you to grow and transform into a mature
Christian and person of discernment.

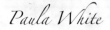
Character

Give us people who are established by principle
rather than moved by passion.

Psalm 119
[11] Thy word have I hid in mine heart, that I might not sin against thee.

_____

_____

_____

_____

_____

Allow God's principles to lead you instead of flesh and "feelings".
True integrity is not gauged by how you feel, but by how God feels.

Character

When I walk in who I am – then I know who I'm not!

Psalm 89:8
8   O LORD God of hosts, who is mighty as thou art, O LORD,
with thy faithfulness round about thee?

_____

_____

_____

_____

_____

Faithfulness is God's character. You have the ability to walk in the character of God as a child of His.

Treasure of the Day   *Paula White*

Character

It is time to move from external control to internal principles.

Job 8
[6] If you were pure and upright, Surely now He would awake for you,
And prosper your rightful dwelling place.

_____

_____

_____

_____

_____

When you are driven by the principles of God inwardly, He will bless your life outwardly.

Character

When you have to debate within yourself to do right or not,
you don't have any principles.

1Kings 9

4 "Now if you walk before Me as your father David walked, in integrity of heart and in uprightness, to do according to all that I have commanded you, and if you keep My statutes and My judgments, 5 "then I will establish the throne of your kingdom over Israel forever, as I promised David your father, saying, 'You shall not fail to have a man on the throne of Israel.'

Follow God in integrity and godliness and He will give you divine discernment between right and wrong.

Character

Things might go wrong, but you don't have to go with them.

Proverbs 10
[9] He who walks with integrity walks securely,
But he who perverts his ways will become known.

_____

_____

_____

_____

_____

In the midst of temptation, those with integrity have firm footing on the Word.
A lack of integrity creates an unstable foundation.

Fear

If you have fear, your love has not been perfected.

1 John 4
18 There is no fear in love; but perfect love casteth out fear: because fear hath torment. He that feareth is not made perfect in love.

_____

_____

_____

_____

_____

Fear is not of God. When you experience fear, rebuke it and seek
God for peace that surpasses all understanding.

Fear

Fear is false evidence appearing real.

Phillipians 4
6 Be anxious for nothing, but in everything by prayer and supplication,
with thanksgiving, let your requests be made known to God;

_____

_____

_____

_____

_____

There is no need to worry when you know that you can petition God to take care of all of your needs.

Character

Jealousy is rooted in fear.

Job 5

2   For wrath kills a foolish man, and envy slays a simple one.

_____

_____

_____

_____

_____

Envy is the fear that something or someone can replace you. When you are confident in your divine birthright through Christ, you are not concerned about anyone else getting the blessings that you deserve.

Fear

Fear means to "take flight".

1 Samuel 12

20   And Samuel said unto the people, Fear not: ye have done all this wickedness: yet turn
not aside from following the LORD, but serve the LORD with all your heart;

_____

_____

_____

_____

_____

Do not run away from God in your fear. That is the perfect time to turn to Him.
Repent for whatever separated you from God, and rest in His reassurance today.

Fear

Fear has torment while faith has rest.

Leviticus 26

6 I will give peace in the land, and you shall lie down, and none will make you afraid; I will rid the land of evil beasts, and the sword will not go through your land.

_____

_____

_____

_____

_____

Faith in God will give you peace so you can rest, free of your concerns.

Fear

Fear, worry and anxiety are interest paid in advance for something you probably will never own.

Luke 1

[74] To grant us that we, Being delivered from the hand of our enemies, Might serve Him without fear,

_____

_____

_____

_____

_____

You have already been rescued from your enemies so there is nothing to fear.

Fear

Panic is groundless fear.

Matthew 10

[28] "And do not fear those who kill the body but cannot kill the soul.
But rather fear Him who is able to destroy both soul and body in hell.

_____

_____

_____

_____

_____

Do not fear man – he can only destroy your temporary body.
Fear only God who is the master of your soul.

Fear

You cannot conquer what you are not willing to confront.

1John 4
[4] You are of God, little children, and have overcome them,
because He who is in you is greater than he who is in the world.

_____

_____

_____

_____

_____

Whatever your fear is, you can overcome it by facing it head on with the power of Christ.
Yield to God and allow Him to remove all fears and obstacles away from you today.

Fear

Don't let God's promises pass you by because you are unwilling to confront the opposition.

Psalm 27

3 Though an host should encamp against me, my heart shall not fear:

5 For in the time of trouble he shall hide me in his pavilion: in the secret of his tabernacle shall he hide me; he shall set me up upon a rock.

_____

_____

_____

_____

_____

The only way you can overcome the opposition is to confront it head on. Trust in the power of God to move the obstacle while taking steps in the direction of God, and He will hide you from the enemy.

Fear

You create the behavior you fear the most.

Job 3

[25] For the thing which I greatly feared is come upon me, and that which
I was afraid of is come unto me.

_____

_____

_____

_____

_____

You must get to the root of where fear would fester in your life.
Cut it out by applying the blood of Jesus to your life and giving it over to Him.

Fear

Fear is Satan's greatest weapon

Genesis 26

[24] And the LORD appeared unto him the same night, and said, I am the God of Abraham thy father: fear not, for I am with thee, and will bless thee, and multiply thy seed for my servant Abraham's sake.

_____

_____

_____

_____

_____

As with all of the enemy's weapons, fear is powerless in the face of God. God is with you always to fight your battles and to protect you from the enemy's snare.

Fear

Do it in the face of fear.

Exodus 14
15 And the Lord said to Moses, Why are you crying out to me?
give the children of Israel the order to go forward.

_____

_____

_____

_____

_____

Whenever you do something great for God, it's normal to feel fear. Just GO FOR IT!

Fear

Your faith will overcome any fear.

Psalm 27:1
¹ The LORD is my light and my salvation; whom shall I fear? t
he LORD is the strength of my life; of whom shall I be afraid?

_____

_____

_____

_____

_____

Perfect faith in God cancels all fear. When you begin to feel anxious, take a moment to reflect on who God is and what He has already delivered out of.

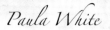
Fear

To have anxiety is to worry about something that has
not happened and may never occur.

Isaiah 35
[4] Say to them that are of a fearful heart, Be strong, fear not:
behold, your God will come with vengeance, even God with a recompence;
He will come and save you.

_____

_____

_____

_____

_____

Do not fear for God is with you and in you.
He has already devoured your enemy and delivered you into safety.

Fear

Most people live their whole lives as complete strangers to themselves.

1Samuel 18

18 And David said unto Saul, Who am I? and what is my life, or my father's family in Israel, that I should be son in law to the king? 23 And Saul's servants spake those words in the ears of David. And David said, Seemeth it to you a light thing to be a king's son in law, seeing that I am a poor man, and lightly esteemed?

_____

_____

_____

_____

_____

David was not able to see himself as a king's son-in-law because He did not fully understand the vision that God had for him. Seek God for revelation about the awesome vision that He has for you today so that you will not limit yourself by your own expectations.

Getting to Know Yourself

Know your weaknesses…your enemy does.

Psalm 89:22

22 The enemy shall not outwit him, Nor the son of wickedness afflict him.

_____

_____

_____

_____

_____

Don't let the enemy outwit you by identifying the areas in which you are vulnerable before you do. When your enemy knows your weak spot, he can attack you in that place and overtake you.

Getting to Know Yourself

Don't let your identity be wrapped up in an item. You are not
defined by what you have but who you are.

Ecclesiastes 5
[10] He that loveth silver shall not be satisfied with silver;
nor he that loveth abundance with increase: this is also vanity.

----

*Materials things will all pass away. Invest in the things of God that will withstand time. It is the
wealth of the spirit that makes you most valuable.*

Getting to Know Yourself

We cannot fully know who we are until we know who God is.

Deuteronomy 7

[9] Know therefore that the LORD thy God, he is God, the faithful God, which keepeth covenant and mercy with them that love him and keep his commandments to a thousand generations;

_____

_____

_____

_____

_____

You are a child of the awesome God who created the earth and stars.
Come into the fullness of who you are through your knowledge of who He is.

Getting to Know Yourself

Don't go where the path may lead. Make a path for yourself.

Ephesians 5
[1] Be ye therefore followers of God, as dear children;

_____

_____

_____

_____

_____

Don't follow the path that man creates;
follow God as He paves a designated path that leads to your destiny!

Getting to Know Yourself

You must know who you are with a vision of who you're becoming.

Proverbs 29

[18] Where there is no vision, the people perish: but he that keepeth the law, happy is he.

_____

_____

_____

_____

_____

Vision is key when thinking about who you are. You are nobody if you are not headed someplace to accomplish something in Christ.

Getting to Know Yourself

Quit comparing yourself to everyone around you and forcing
yourself to do what they're doing.

Galatians 6

4 But let every man prove his own work, and then shall he have rejoicing in himself
alone, and not in another.

5 For every man shall bear his own burden.

_____

_____

_____

_____

_____

Each of us will be accountable for ourselves when we face God on judgment day.
You have to work out your own salvation.
Seek God to know what He expects of you so that you can get busy achieving your personal destiny.

Getting to Know Yourself

If people don't know what your passion is, you don't have one.

John 2

17 And it came to the minds of the disciples that the Writings say,
I am on fire with passion for your house.

What would you do for free if you didn't need to work? That is where your passion lies.
Take some time to explore your personal passions and seek God to help you
carve those into personal goals and accomplishments.

Getting to Know Yourself

You will never know what's in you if you dwell in the
darkness of yesterday.

Isaiah 60
[1] Arise, shine; For your light has come! And the glory of the LORD is risen upon you.

_____

_____

_____

_____

_____

*Let go of the past and step into the future that God has for you. Each time you take a step towards
your future, God moves your future blessings closer to you. There is an incredible person inside of you
who can't wait to "Arise and Shine".*

Getting to Know Yourself

It takes a lot of energy and effort to try to be someone else.
Be you!

1 Colossians 8

⁴ But to us there is but one God, the Father, of whom are all things, and we in him;
and one Lord Jesus Christ, by whom are all things, and we by him.

_____

_____

_____

_____

_____

As child of the only true living God, you are perfectly unique and called to a unique purpose. Don't waste any energy trying to be anyone else, when you could just be a wonderful You.

Getting to Know Yourself

Those around you have a way of defining "who" you are by "what" you did.

2 Corinthians 5

¹⁷ Therefore if any man be in Christ, he is a new creature: old things are passed away; behold, all things are become new.

_____

_____

_____

_____

_____

Although people identify you by what you do, God sees your heart and your thoughts before He takes note of your outward actions. When you receive Jesus as your personal Lord and Savior, you become a new creation. Build a new life in Christ.

Getting to Know Yourself

When you know "who" you are, you don't have to struggle to live up to what someone has defined you to be.

1 John 5

¹ Whosoever believeth that Jesus is the Christ is born of God: and every one that loveth him that begat loveth him also that is begotten of him.

_____

_____

_____

_____

_____

Once you realize "whose" you are, you will be confident that you can achieve anything you set your thoughts on.

Getting to Know Yourself

Don't spend a lifetime trying to be what you were not created to be.

Romans 8

[28] And we know that all things work together for good to them that love God, to them who are the called according to his purpose.

_____

_____

_____

_____

_____

You have been created for a purpose – God's purpose.
Life is too short to waste time not working at the very thing you have been created to do.

Getting to Know Yourself

If you don't know where you are, you're unstable, and it is
difficult to then see the absolutes or sovereignty of God.

James 1
[8] A double minded man is unstable in all his ways.

_____

_____

_____

_____

_____

Instability is a hindrance to your walk with God.
If you don't know which way to go, lean on God and He will direct you.

Restoration

God restores the depleted areas in life.

2 Samuel 9

[7] And David said unto him, Fear not: for I will surely shew thee kindness for Jonathan thy father's sake, and will restore thee all the land of Saul thy father; and thou shalt eat bread at my table continually.

_____

_____

_____

_____

_____

Trust God for replenishment of all that the enemy has taken away from you. He will fill every void with His love.

Restoration

Restoration requires a stripping down to the original.

Revelation 2

[5] Remember therefore from whence thou art fallen, and repent, and do t he first works; or else I will come unto thee quickly, and will remove thy candlestick out of his place, except thou repent.

In order to be spiritually restored, you must first remember the condition you were in before you wandered away from God. God will cut off all the "debris" that you have picked up along the way to get down to the Real You and restore you from the inside out.

Restoration

After you pass through the pain and sorrow, God will always
appoint a time of healing and restoration for you.

Ecclesiastes 3

¹ To every thing there is a season, and a time to every purpose under the heaven:

³ A time to kill, and a time to heal; a time to break down, and a time to build up;

Stand firm in the knowledge that God has already determined the end from the beginning. As you seek
His face, He will heal your wounds and dissolve your pain.

Restoration

God has placed His strength where your weakness was.

2 Corinthians 12
⁹ And he said unto me, My grace is sufficient for thee:
for my strength is made perfect in weakness.

_____

_____

_____

_____

_____

When you have lost all strength and you feel as if you have no more to give,
it's in the Father's mighty bosom that you will find rest.
His perfect strength will empower you to endure more than you ever could alone.

Restoration

God will give you double for all of your trouble.

Isaiah 61

⁶ But ye shall be named the Priests of the LORD: men shall call
you the Ministers of our God: ye shall eat the riches of the Gentiles,
and in their glory shall ye boast yourselves.

⁷ For your shame ye shall have double; and for confusion they shall rejoice in their
portion: therefore in their land they shall possess the double: everlasting joy shall be
unto them.

_____

_____

_____

_____

_____

Get ready to take back from the enemy all that was ever taken from you, with interest!

Restoration

If you take Jesus to the place you were "buried," He will raise the dead man.

John 11

[34] And said, Where have ye laid him? They said unto him, Lord, come and see.
[43] And when he thus had spoken, he cried with a loud voice, Lazarus, come forth.
[44] And he that was dead came forth…

Allow Jesus to touch those deep places within you that you have shut off from the world. It is there where he will restore you and heal wounds that you have hidden from others all your life.

Restoration

Did you know God was preaching a gospel sermon through your life?

Acts 20

[24] But none of these things move me, neither count I my life dear unto myself, so that I might finish my course with joy, and the ministry, which I have received of the Lord Jesus, to testify the gospel of the grace of God.

_____

_____

_____

_____

_____

Use the story of your deliverance to testify to others about the grace of God.
Start proclaiming your testimony while you are still in the test.

Restoration

When people are finished with you, God is just getting started.

1 Samuel 16

[7] …for the LORD seeth not as man seeth; for man looketh on the outward appearance, but the LORD looketh on the heart.

_____

_____

_____

_____

_____

Sometimes man is not able to see the beautiful you that God sees. He who knew you before you were in your mother's womb will always see beauty where others see ashes.

Restoration

From the wholeness of your relationship with Jesus, you can regain the courage to experience love and life with others.

1 John 4

7 Beloved, let us love one another: for love is of God; and every one that loveth is born of God, and knoweth God.

_____

_____

_____

_____

_____

Allow yourself to share the gift of love that God has so liberally shared with you.

Restoration

A person with a past can touch a God in the present who is able to change the future.

Titus 3

5 Not by works of righteousness which we have done, but according to his mercy he saved us, by the washing of regeneration, and renewing of the Holy Ghost;

_____

_____

_____

_____

_____

Because of God's sovereign ability to see beyond our past, we can walk boldly into our future with a renewed body, mind, and spirit.

Restoration

Deliverance means that the thing that used to control you is now under control.

2 Timothy 1

[7] For God hath not given us the spirit of fear; but of power, and of love, and of a sound mind.

_____

_____

_____

_____

_____

To have a sound mind means to have self-control and discipline. Praise God for delivering you from bondage, restoring what the enemy stole, and freeing your mind to serve Him with all that you are!

Restoration

A person with a past can touch a God in the present
who is able to change the future.

Titus 3

5 Not by works of righteousness which we have done, but according to his mercy he
saved us, by the washing of regeneration, and renewing of the Holy Ghost;

_____

_____

_____

_____

_____

Because of God's sovereign ability to see beyond our past,
we can walk boldly into our future with a renewed body, mind, and spirit.

Restoration

Deliverance means that the thing that used to control you is now under control.

2 Timothy 1

7 For God hath not given us the spirit of fear; but of power, and of love, and of a sound mind.

_____

_____

_____

_____

_____

To have a sound mind means to have self-control and discipline. Praise God for delivering you from bondage, restoring what the enemy stole, and freeing your mind to serve Him with all that you are!

Restoration

Damaged but still delivered.

Psalm 94
[19] In the multitude of my thoughts within me thy comforts delight my soul.

When I was wrought with anxiety, His consolation brought joy to my soul and now I am whole again.

Restoration

If God can get over your past, why can't you get beyond it?

Isaiah 43

[18] Remember ye not the former things, neither consider the things of old.

_____

_____

_____

_____

_____

Today is the first day of the best days of your life. Declare today to never look back on where you came from, except to testify about where you are today!

Restoration

God does his finest works in the lives of broken people.

Psalm 147
³ He healeth the broken in heart, and bindeth up their wounds.

_____

_____

_____

_____

_____

God specializes in your infirmity. Whatever the hurt, he is the Mighty Physician!

Marriage & Family

Submission is for your safety.

Colossians 3:18

[18] Wives, submit to your own husbands, as is fitting in the Lord.

Submission is a principle provided by God to protect us and maintain order. To submit means to "duck down" and get out of the way so God can step in and fix the situation.

Marriage & Family

You should be a platform for your children to build on.

John 13

[15] For I have given you an example, that ye should do as I have done to you.

_____

_____

_____

_____

_____

Just as Jesus was an example for you to follow, so should you be for your children. Being an effective role model for your children comes as you fashion yourselves after the model of Christ.

Marriage & Family

What you do to catch a spouse is what you'll have to continue
doing to keep them.

Mark 10

[19] Thou knowest the commandments, Do not commit adultery, Do not kill, Do not
steal, Do not bear false witness, Defraud not, Honour thy father and mother.

_____

_____

_____

_____

_____

*If in your quest to find a spouse, you resort to breaking commandments of God, that relationship will
be overshadowed by that sin. Being driven by the flesh is dangerous because the flesh is never satisfied.
Ask God to restore your relationship to be healthy and whole, and free from fleshly motives.*

Marriage & Family

Parenting, whether proper or improper, shapes a child's future.

Proverbs 22
6 Train up a child in the way he should go:
and when he is old, he will not depart from it.

_____

_____

_____

_____

_____

Proper child rearing results in children maturing into responsible adults. On that same token, what you impart into your child in a negative way will stay with them throughout their life and always affect the way the view the world and you.

Marriage & Family

It is normal to have contradicting opinions – it is dangerous to be led by them.

Matthew 12
[25] And Jesus knew their thoughts, and said unto them,
Every kingdom divided against itself is brought to desolation;
and every city or house divided against itself shall not stand:

_____

_____

_____

_____

_____

Learn to disagree with your spouse in a way that provides each of you the opportunity to express your viewpoints without fear of insult. Pray before you have tough discussions, asking God to step in and help you control your emotions and your tongues.

Marriage & Family

Many married women can't become a queen, because they won't give up being a princess.

2 Samuel 6

23 Therefore Michal the daughter of Saul had no child unto the day of her death.

Michal, the first wife and love of King David, became the sad seed of a bitter critical father. You must leave your past behind when you come into a new covenant of marriage.

Marriage & Family

When bringing correction, use the sandwich technique:
(+) positive (-) negative (+) positive.

Proverbs 10

[17]   He who keeps instruction is in the way of life,
But he who refuses correction goes astray.

_____

_____

_____

_____

_____

The proper way to bring correction is to accompany it with encouragement and support. Telling the person what they are doing well in addition to the criticism balances out the discussion by giving them a feeling of accomplishment along with the opportunity for development.

Marriage & Family

If you are single and wanting to be married, God is making
you a "good thing" to be found.

Proverbs 18

22 He who finds a wife finds a good thing, And obtains favor from the LORD.

Trust in God that He is preparing you to be a fitting spouse for when He brings your mate along.
Cherish every opportunity to grow and mature into a "good thing" along the way.

Marriage & Family

Your imagination needs stimulation of association with significant others.

1 Corinthians 15
[33] Be not deceived: evil communications corrupt good manners.

_____

_____

_____

_____

_____

You become a product of what you are around.

Marriage & Family

When you continually criticize a child, it drives them to perfectionism or depression.

Psalm 69

[20] Insults and reproach have broken my heart; I am full of heaviness and I am distressingly sick. I looked for pity, but there was none, and for comforters, but I found none. (AMP)

_____

_____

_____

_____

_____

Extreme discipline is dangerous to the self-esteem and mental welfare of a child. Be especially careful of the words you speak into the fragile life of a child. Pray before speaking in anger and ask God to guide you in bringing correction.

Marriage & Family

Conduct permitted is conduct approved.

Proverbs 22
[15] Foolishness is bound in the heart of a child;
but the rod of correction shall drive it far from him.

_____

_____

_____

_____

_____

Be firm about what you accept from your children so they will know your boundaries as a parent.
Constructive criticism and correction in love will be valuable to the growth of your child.

Marriage & Family

Make memories with those you love.

Ecclesiastes 9

[9] Live joyfully with the wife whom you love all the days of your vain life which He has given you under the sun--all the days of futility. For that is your portion in this life and in your work at which you toil under the sun.

_____

_____

_____

_____

_____

Spend time with those you love to enjoy their company and build relationship through creating happy memories that will last a lifetime.

Marriage & Family

You cannot hold others to a standard you
are unwilling to live for yourself.

Hebrews 5

[12] For even though by this time you ought to be teaching others, you actually need someone to teach you over again the very first principles of God's Word. You have come to need milk, not solid food. (AMP)

_____

_____

_____

_____

_____

Are you living a life that is exemplary?
How can you be an example to follow if you still need to be trained in the gospel?
Be sure to mature in the Word and continue to grow as you train up your family in your footsteps.

Marriage & Family

People change – but not much.

Jeremiah 13

23 Can the Ethiopian change his skin, or the leopard his spots? then may ye also do good, that are accustomed to do evil.

_____

_____

_____

_____

_____

God can transform people and make them new with His restoration power.
But it is up to each man to maintain that change and not return to their evil ways.
That is a choice we all make each day – to progress or regress.

Provision

When you give birth to your promise, it will attract resources
to sustain its growth.

Matthew 2

[11] And when they were come into the house, they saw the young child with Mary his
mother, and fell down, and worshipped him: and when they had opened their treasures,
they presented unto him gifts; gold, and frankincense, and myrrh.

---

*When Jesus was born, there came wise men bearing gifts. This is a great example of how God's
provision appears just when you need it. When you are in line with God's will, the provision will come.*

Provision

There are resources that have been put in the hands of "wise men" who will watch over and protect that which will sustain you – until its appointed time.

2 Kings 7

1 THEN ELISHA said, Hear the word of the Lord. Thus says the Lord: Tomorrow about this time a measure of fine flour will sell for a shekel and two measures of barley for a shekel in the gate of Samaria!

2 Then the captain on whose hand the king leaned answered the man of God and said, If the Lord should make windows in heaven, could this thing be? But Elisha said, You shall see it with your own eyes, but you shall not eat of it. (AMP).

_____

_____

_____

_____

_____

What a mighty God we serve! He has riches stored up for you,
just waiting for the right time to bless you with them!

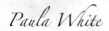
Provision

God is your source – He uses many different resources.

Ephesians 3

[20] Now unto him that is able to do exceeding abundantly above all that we ask or think, according to the power that worketh in us.

When you depend on God to provide all of your needs and desires, He will make His riches available to you through means that you may never expect.

356

Treasure of the Day

Paula White

Provision

When God calls you, He equips you.

Hebrews 13:20

[20] Now the God of peace, that brought again from the dead our Lord Jesus, that great shepherd of the sheep, through the blood of the everlasting covenant,

[21] Make you perfect in every good work to do his will, working in you that which is well-pleasing in his sight, through Jesus Christ; to whom be glory for ever and ever. Amen.

God will grant you the peace of God and the power to achieve anything he calls you to do. Once you submit to His will, all you will need to fulfill His promise will come.

Provision

God gives the good things that the wicked want.

Proverbs 13

[22] A good man leaveth an inheritance to his children's children:
and the wealth of the sinner is laid up for the just.

_____

_____

_____

_____

_____

*God can make a divine transferal of assets from sinners to the righteous. When we please God, He
uses ways that are beyond our imagination to turn situations around to work in our favor.*

Provision

God will never give you a vision without provision.

Matthew 6

[33] But seek ye first the kingdom of God, and his righteousness; and all these things shall be added unto you.

_____

_____

_____

_____

_____

If God has shown you a mighty vision to achieve, you can rest assured that He will bless you with all the resources you will need to make it come to pass.

Provision

Poverty is not just a condition or a state of being.
It's a mindset.

Luke 6:38
[38] Give, and it shall be given unto you; good measure, pressed down,
and shaken together, and running over, shall men give into your bosom.
For with the same measure that ye mete withal it shall be measured to you again.

_____

_____

_____

_____

_____

The key to receiving God's provision is obedience. You must give in order to receive.
The way to break the spirit of poverty over your life is to learn to sow into God's kingdom.
Your seed will come back as your provision.

Provision

God gives you ways to prosper.

Philippians 4

[19] But my God shall supply all your needs according to his riches in glory by Christ Jesus.

God has income streams just waiting for you to tap into. As long as you sow, He will provide ways for you to reap.

Provision

You please God when you walk in His prosperity.

Job 36
[11] If they obey and serve Him, They shall spend their days in prosperity,
And their years in pleasures

_____

_____

_____

_____

_____

What a thought that is! To walk in God's prosperity is beyond any prosperity that man can offer.
HIS prosperity touches all areas of our lives –
including relationships, finances, health and spiritual prosperity.

Provision

Nothing ever leaves you hand that does not enter your future.

Genesis 8

22   While the earth remaineth, seedtime and harvest, and cold and heat, and summer and winter, and day and night shall not cease.

_____

_____

_____

_____

_____

The principle of Seedtime and Harvest is absolute. It is a constant that will remain as long as we remain on earth. The more you give, the more you will receive.

Provision

You don't have a provision problem but a revelation problem.

Ecclesistes 3

[14] I know that, whatsoever God doeth, it shall be forever: nothing can be put to it, nor any thing taken from it: and God doeth it, that men should fear before him.

_____

_____

_____

_____

_____

Your issue is not with God's provision, but with your ability to recognize the provision.
What God has destined for you will be, and nothing can change it.
Take a moment today to look around and see what the Lord has done!

Favorite Treasure

_____

_____

_____

_____

_____

_____

_____

_____

_____

_____

_____

_____

_____

_____

Favorite Treasure

_____

_____

_____

_____

_____

_____

_____

_____

_____

_____

_____

_____

_____

Favorite Treasure

_____

_____

_____

_____

_____

_____

_____

_____

_____

_____

_____

_____

_____

_____

_____

Favorite Treasure

_____

_____

_____

_____

_____

_____

_____

_____

_____

_____

_____

_____

Favorite Treasure

_____

_____

_____

_____

_____

_____

_____

_____

_____

_____

_____

_____

_____

_____

Favorite Treasure

_____

_____

_____

_____

_____

_____

_____

_____

_____

_____

_____

_____

_____

_____

Favorite Treasure

_____

_____

_____

_____

_____

_____

_____

_____

_____

_____

_____

_____

_____

Favorite Treasure

_____

_____

_____

_____

_____

_____

_____

_____

_____

_____

_____

_____

_____

_____

Favorite Treasure

Favorite Treasure

Favorite Treasure

_____

_____

_____

_____

_____

_____

_____

_____

_____

_____

_____

_____

_____

_____

Favorite Treasure